Knowledge
and Ignorance in
Economics

Knowledge and Ignorance in Economics

T.W. Hutchison

THE UNIVERSITY OF CHICAGO PRESS

Published 1977
The University of Chicago Press, Chicago 60637
Basil Blackwell, Oxford, OX1 4HB

83 82 81 80 79 78 77 4321

Library of Congress Cataloging in Publication Data

Hutchison, Terence Wilmot.
  Knowledge and ignorance in economics.

  Includes index.
    1. Economics. 2. Economics – Methodology.
1. Title.
HB71.H799   1977   330   76–54771
ISBN 0–226–36236–1

Printed in Great Britain

Contents

Acknowledgments

Section III has appeared in a volume of papers entitled *Method and Appraisal in Economics*, edited by Dr. S. J. Latsis and published by the Cambridge University Press. These papers were given at, or emerged from, the Nafplion Colloquium of September 1974 on Research Programmes in Physics and Economics. I would like to express my cordial thanks to the organisers and especially to Dr. Latsis. The version of this paper which appears here is slightly amended.

I would also like to take this opportunity of expressing my gratitude for generous hospitality received when delivering earlier or partial versions of other sections of this book, and especially to Professor Douglas Vickers and Dr. Robin Ghosh, and their colleagues, of the Economics Department of the University of Western Australia; to Professor Tamotsu Matsuura of Keio University, Tokyo; and to Professor R. Richter of the University of the Saarland.

I am also very grateful to Diana Sheedy for her work on the typescript.

The Master said: 'Yu! Shall I teach you the meaning of knowledge? When you know a thing to recognize that you know it; and when you do not, to know that you do not know – that is knowledge'. Confucius THE ANALECTS, translated by W. E. Soothill.

One
Introduction

*One may properly feel that the first discipline
any student, beginning a degree, in any faculty,
should learn is just what the sciences can do
and especially what they cannot do.*
A. L. Macfie THE INDIVIDUAL IN SOCIETY,
1967, p. 13.

It might be taken as a sign of intellectual provincialism, or parochialism, to claim that one's own particular academic backyard possesses some specially intriguing interest or significance. But the philosophical or methodological problems of economics do occupy a rather special, or peculiar, position. Claimed to be the most 'effective' or 'mature' of the social or human sciences, or described as the 'hardest' of the 'soft' sciences, economics seems destined for a somewhat ambiguous and problematic place in the spectrum of knowledge.

The main problems of the methodology of economics revolve around its body of what is called 'theory', the possession of which is held to mark off the subject from other less 'developed' social sciences – though this 'theory', or quasi-theory – would sometimes, or usually, more suitably be described as 'analysis', or perhaps as 'theorems'.[1]* For it is constructed,

* Notes are to be found at the end of the text (pp. 144 ff).

to a large extent, on the basis of a high degree of abstraction or simplification, as is also much of the quantification, or proxy-quantification, in economics, which often also involves a crucial degree of abstraction.

Any methodological assessment of a subject should consider its *aims*. So the question follows as to what 'fruit', relevant to real-world policies, in the form of predictions, or in some other practically significant form (if there is one) can or does eventually emerge from such drastic processes of abstraction, however rigorous or refined these may be. For although, following Ricardo, many economists have resorted to high, and ever higher, degrees of abstraction and simplification in their analysis, they have almost invariably held to, and proclaimed, on the other hand, the aim or criterion of *ultimate*, practical, fruit-bearing policy-relevance, in terms of promoting the wealth and welfare of nations.[2] In fact, David Ricardo MP, the great pioneer of drastic unrestricted abstraction or simplification in economic analysis, is the classic, historical embodiment of a kind of deep-seated methodological paradox, or tension, in the subject. For Ricardo did not go into Parliament to deliver academic lectures of no policy relevance, but with the confident claim that his 'new science', though based on drastic abstraction or 'strong cases' (i.e. extremely over-simplified cases), nevertheless had great and immediate contributions to offer to the guidance and enlightenment of economic policy-making.

It remains a continuing paradox in economics that in spite of the great prestige of what has been called 'high theory', or work based on the most refined and extreme abstractions and simplifications, it nevertheless often seems to be felt necessary to justify this kind of activity by claiming for it some actual, or *eventual*, policy-relevance, or even 'very great practical importance'.[3] Indeed it seems that to deny 'practical importance', or real-world relevance, to an economist's work is usually taken to be a damning charge which it is vital to refute. However, the practical importance and relevance that is claimed is sometimes seen only as an optimistically promised, or hoped-for one, which will, it is trusted, emerge eventually, 'at the end of the day', from current 'theoretical' constructions, when all the supporting, simplificatory 'scaffolding' is, at some future date, removed. Meanwhile, it seems difficult for economists, however drastic the abstractions and simplifications in which they indulge, to abandon explicitly the traditional aims and claims of fruit-bearing policy-relevance, which have come down from the 'mercantilists' and 'consultant administrators', through Adam Smith and the classicals, Marshall and Keynes.

In assessing such aims and claims regarding fruit-bearing policy-relevance, questions regarding prediction in economics are crucially important: questions, that is, as to how far prediction is an attainable (and attained) objective, and, if it is not, just how, if at all, economists have contributed, or can claim to be able to contribute, to less unsuccessful policy-making, which they so often seem to have assumed to be the main objective of their efforts. Views about the kind of subject economics is, and about the nature of economic knowledge, must be related rather closely to views regarding the capacity to predict in economics.

Anyhow, the would-be, 'great practical importance', or close policy-relevance, which seems usually to be claimed, or aimed at, by economists, also gives rise to much-debated questions of the precise relations between economics and ethics, or politics, or of the nature of the value-judgments which have to be, or are, made by economists. Moreover this often assumed policy-relevance leads on to a second major reason for studying, and seeking more clarity regarding, the nature and extent of economic knowledge and ignorance. For the methodological and epistemological nature and status of economics is not merely an intriguing philosophical or scholarly subject (though that alone, of course, would be quite sufficient to justify its place in academic studies). *Questions of the extent and limits of economic knowledge and ignorance can be of great social and political importance* (and probably have been in Britain in the nineteen-sixties and seventies). For political processes and institutions have been under serious strain partly because people and politicians are dominated by quite excessive expectations as to what can possibly, or practicably, be delivered by governmental economic policies. A clear grasp of what economic policies can reasonably be expected to achieve, or deliver, and what they cannot, depends, in turn, on a clear grasp of the extent and limits of economic knowledge and ignorance. It has become almost endemic for professional politicians to promise more than can be performed. But some economists in Britain, in the last decade or two, instead of trying to counter the arousal of excessive expectations, have rather contributed to the process: for example, with regard to how far, by means of controls on incomes, 'full' (or 'over-full') employment could be combined with a not-too-serious rate of inflation; and also regarding how far the rate of economic growth could be raised by 'purposive' action and direction by governments. The encouragement of such excessive expectations was based on fundamental misconceptions regarding the nature and significance of recent would-be contributions (often in the form of extremely abstract model-building) to economic knowledge regarding processes of 'growth'. Often dissatisfaction has been stirred up with a level of performance of the economy (e.g. in respect of employment) which it may have been very dangerous, or costly, to try to improve upon. The disappointment of unnecessarily stimulated expectations or illusions, among politicians and people, might have serious political consequences.[4]

The naively Utopian, scientist expectations of the early twentieth century regarding the blessings for mankind which would flow from the progress of the natural sciences have now long since faded away behind threatening mushroom-shaped clouds. But very naive expectations seem still to be quite widespread regarding the blessings for human welfare, prosperity, and happiness, which may be expected from the development of the social sciences, including economics. The point is not simply that such expected blessings might well prove illusory, *even if some great leap forward in economic knowledge were to take place* (such as *has* taken place, for example, in the last half-century in physics). The point is that, in any case, no such great leap forward can reasonably be expected. Meanwhile, no kind of ignorance can be more dangerous than ignorance regarding the limits and limitations of one's knowledge. In so far as he may be able to combat and reduce this kind of ignorance, the student of the methodology and history of economics has a task which is of considerable social and political importance, as well as a worthy scholarly and philosophically interesting pursuit. *In fact, to promote clarification of the extent and limits of economic knowledge and ignorance may well do much more to reduce dissatisfaction with current economic policies and their results, than do many or most of the contributions to confused and undisciplined wrangles and debates on particular policy problems.* Discerning and emphasising limitations may not seem very warmly inspiring or exciting as a message. But economists are only preparing disappointment and disillusionment for politicians, the public, and themselves, if they demand, like prophets, to be fired by impressive or exciting inspirations. Rather they should be prepared to follow the contrasting comparison suggested by Keynes: 'If economists could manage to get themselves thought of as humble, competent people, on a level with dentists, that would be splendid'.[5]

The arousal of excessive expectations is also dangerous at the level of student beginners. In these days, when the fate of academic empires may depend on pulling in the crowds, there may be a tendency (discernible in some textbooks) to oversell economics, both in terms of its 'scientific' character, as compared with physics or chemistry, and in terms of the contributions it can make to less unsuccessful policy-making in the real world. The dangers exist, either of the exaggerated claims being swallowed, or of their being reacted against excessively in terms of a crude nihilism.

A good deal has been written about the need for economists to bring the limitations of their theorising into clearer focus by setting out more fully and explicitly their assumptions and biases – as though this was easily done. Regarding the kinds of political bias most often complained of, by one side or the other, each party has now developed such a keen nose for its opponents' biases as to sniff out and protest at any trace of them, even when they are comparatively trivial or easy to discount. But the most dangerous latent assumptions and biases are often those that are shared by economists of *all* schools and parties, by 'orthodox'' and anti-'orthodox', by confident classical liberals, as well as by know-all 'Marxists', by dogmatic, non-mathematical a-priorists, as well as by pretentiously optimistic quantifiers.

These generally held, latent assumptions and biases are not attacked nearly as persistently and indignantly as are the political biases of one or the other rival party. What is shared among economists of very differing parties and schools is an excessive confidence regarding *some one particular brand* of economic theorising and its possibilities. But, of course, each school, party or group, entertains such pretensions *only* regarding *its own* particular theories, doctrines, or methods, while maintaining the most thorough-going scepticism, often well-justified but sometimes even rather exaggerated, regarding the doctrines of other parties, methods, or schools. In fact, excessive claims are indulged in not on behalf of the whole range of partly conflicting doctrines which comprise the subject as a whole, but on behalf of the theories or methods of *one particular school or type* of economics. A magnificent scepticism is often in evidence with regard to *the other brands*: such as 'neoclassicism' or institutionalism; the 'orthodox' or the 'flatearthers'; the 'conventional wisdom' or the 'cranks'; the 'amateurs' or the 'academics'. But this scepticism is often only skin-deep, being matched by a naive overconfidence regarding one particular approved line.

If economics is to be not too unsuccessfully applied to policy it has to be with a clear regard to its limitations, which requires some grasp of the history and philosophy of the subject; and this can only be cultivated and inculcated in universities. What Professor Jacob Viner said with regard to successful teaching in his 'Modest Proposal for some Stress on Scholarship in

Graduate Training', applies just as much to the successful application of economic theorising to policy-making:

> Men who have been trained to think only within the limits of one subject, or only from the point of view of one subject, will never make good teachers at the college level even in that subject. They may know exceedingly well the possibilities of that subject, but they will never be conscious of its limitations, or if conscious of them will never have an adequate motive or a good basis for judging as to their consequences or extent.[6]

Two

On Prediction and Economic Knowledge

I

The question of prediction in economics involves, or brings together, most of the main questions as to what sort of subject economics is: questions, that is, of what economists can or should try or claim to do, and what it is presumptuous, pretentious, or even dangerous and damaging, for them to try or claim to do: questions of what it is reasonable, and what it is fantastic or Utopian to expect in the way of progress in economic knowledge. The course we shall be trying to pick out through this problematic terrain is one which will refrain from over-optimistic comparisons, or assumptions implying something like epistemological parity with the more mature natural sciences in terms of predictive capacity, while on the other hand, avoiding an excessive or nihilistic anti-rational scepticism which would maintain that prediction is 'impossible' for economists.

Perhaps a majority of economists – but not all – would agree that improved predictions of economic behaviour or events is the main or primary task of the economist.[1] It might well be argued that it is *only* by improved predictions that economics, as a would-be 'fruit-bearing', subject, can make a valid contribution to less unsuccessful policy-making. This might be regarded as going a little too far. But if an economist wishes to claim that, though unable to predict, he can nevertheless fruitfully contribute to policy-making, the onus would seem to be upon him to spell out pretty precisely just what such a contribution would consist of.[2] It could be maintained that, without any ability to predict, the economist *first* can identify and describe problems; and *secondly* that he can help elucidate the choice of objectives; and that these are two useful and even essential contributions to successful decision-making. But if the economist *cannot go on to predict at all, or improve or assist in forming less inaccurate predictions, as to the effects of possible policies by which objectives can be approached, then his contribution hardly matches up to the traditional aims and claims to promote the wealth of nations and reduce poverty and unemployment.* A doctor might confidently proclaim (1) that his patient's temperature was 102; and (2) that it 'ought' to be 98.4 (and with *much* more confidence and precision than the economist, *mutatis mutandis*, can usually claim). But if the doctor was quite unable to prognose or predict at all as to the means by which a more desired temperature, or physical condition, could be reached from a less desired one, then the claims which could be made on behalf of medical science would be extremely restricted compared with what they justifiably are.[3]

Certainly if all economic action or behaviour was totally unpredictable, policy-making could only be sheer guess-work. It could only be claimed that *given* a certain 'natural', pre- or non-scientific capacity to predict, the economist, without being able to improve on this 'natural' capacity, might nevertheless be able to elucidate the logical implications of pre- or non-scientific predictive judgments or hunches.

One can therefore only state the task of economics in terms of *improved* prediction, because we are endowed initially with a certain inborn or inbred capacity to predict human and social as well as physical and natural phenomena, before we try to add to, or improve on, or extend this basic capacity by systematic, or 'scientific', intellectual effort. To justify itself in terms of its predictive contribution economics must improve on our basic, informal, 'pre-scientific' capacity to predict or foresee one another's economic behaviour. For virtually *any* economic or social life or co-operation, other than the most 'nasty, brutish, and short', would be impossible if all human behaviour, individually and in aggregates, was completely unpredictable.

However, there appears to be a significant minority of economists who would deny that prediction is a possible objective for economists, or who would maintain that economists' predictions are, and are likely to continue to be, so inaccurate that it is presumptuous, and perhaps even dangerous, to assume the task of attempting prediction. For example, it has been argued that what is described as

> *the impossibility of prediction in economics* follows from the fact that economic change is linked to change in knowledge and future knowledge cannot be gained before its time.[4]

It is not clear what is meant here by 'impossibility', since we are attempting, not entirely unsuccessfully, to predict one another's behaviour every day. If it means that economists cannot and will never be able to predict with the very high degrees of probability and accuracy which many natural scientists can achieve for their predictions, this seems a true and important proposition. Alternatively, when it is stated that prediction is 'impossible', it may simply be meant that it is impossible, by some kind of systematic or 'scientific' study of economics, to improve on such informal, unsystematic, pre-scientific capacity as we possess to predict one another's behaviour. But insisting on the 'impossibility' of prediction in economics seems to be a misleading way of presenting such arguments.

Views opposed to prediction in the social sciences have sometimes been based on a libertarian philosophical insistence that, to be free, behaviour must be essentially unpredictable, and that either if one believes individuals to be 'free', or if one wants them to remain 'free', one must reject the possibility, and/or the desirability, of predicting their behaviour.[5]

It could be argued here that – apart from some ambiguity regarding possibility and desirability – there is a confusion between two dichotomies: 'free' and 'unfree' (or coerced) behaviour; and that between predictable (or predicted) and unpredictable (or unpredicted) behaviour. These are two distinct and different dichotomies, although they do, to a large extent, overlap. But predictable behaviour *might* be free, and unpredictable behaviour might be coerced. Of course there may often be a danger of the prediction of human behaviour being used for coercion and manipulation, or that people may be coerced in order to make their actions predictable. If you want to make someone's behaviour in some ways less unpredictable, putting him in prison, dosing him with drugs, or shooting him, may achieve this. A great deal of opposition to the aim of increasing predictive power regarding human behaviour is based on the fear that this increased power may be used for manipulation or coercion. Prediction has been described, for example, by Marcuse as 'an indispensable tool in the hands of the powers that be'.

This is a justifiable fear. On the other hand, there may be profound dangers to human freedom and well-being stemming from the *un*predictability of human behaviour. In any case, this is a question of the *desirability* of improved prediction as distinct from its *possibility*. It is, however, notable how often desirability and possibility are wished together by economists. If they desire an economy mainly based on 'planning' they will hold the necessary kinds of prediction to be possible or feasible while condemning as impossible the kinds necessary to sustain the smooth working of free markets: *vice versa* for those who desire an economy based mainly on free markets. In fact, though there may be much general or abstract agreement among economists regarding the possibility of improved predictions, this will conceal very wide differences as to *the kinds* of predictions the improvement of which are regarded as feasible, or which should be attempted.

There is also profound scepticism regarding prediction and predictability in economics, which does not derive from a libertarian philosophical viewpoint, but simply from a highly critical assessment of the record of attempted economic predictions. For example, Professor R. Clower has written: 'If successful prediction were the sole criterion of a science, economics should long have ceased to exist as a serious intellectual pursuit'.[6]

But we shall not examine further what, among economists, seems to be a minority view. We propose to continue on the assumption, which tentatively and with reservations seems acceptable, that to improve prediction or forecasting in one way or another, or to prevent prediction deteriorating, is, and should be, a main aim of economists and that it is *to some limited extent* a feasible aim. It may be noted that we are not here distinguishing between 'prediction', 'forecasting', 'prognostication', or 'projection'. Various distinctions can be drawn between these but they do not significantly or essentially affect the main epistemological points with which we are here concerned, because the same root difficulties apply to both 'prediction' and 'forecasting' in so far as these are actually being applied to policy decisions in the real world.

II

Until quite recently very little had been written by English economists about the problems of prediction. But whenever economists have applied their theories to policy as, of course, they have constantly tried to do, in so far as their contributions have not been purely normative, or persuasive, or devoted to preaching and propaganda, *some kind* of prediction must presumably have been made (if it was indeed a genuine *'theory'* which was being applied).[7] Until recent decades these predictions have mostly been very rough qualitative predictive judgments, derived from fairly imprecise qualitative pseudo-laws, or generalisations, and initial conditions or assumptions, checked mainly by casual impressionist estimation. Sometimes such predictions could not be, or were not, set out sufficiently precisely to be seriously tested, even if adequate statistics or evidence had been available – which they often were not.[8]

In any case, until fifty years or so ago, there was, compared with today, very little effective demand from government or business for more precise predictions or forecasts. On the more operational side of public policy the main demands on predictive capacity did not go far beyond what was required roughly to balance a comparatively very small budget (though there was also the need to set up and maintain the institutional framework for a free-market economy). On the side of pricing and distribution, or micro-economics, a predictive challenge could hardly have been felt very keenly with most of the staple models often based on assumptions of correct foresight, or correct expectations, that is, of economic units generally predicting correctly *anyway*, without any help from the economist. In fact, in so far as he relied upon 'models' in which individuals predicted correctly, the economist may have been inclined towards rather over-optimistic assumptions about his own ability and need to predict.

It was the business cycle, or 'Juglar' cycle, which really stimulated the demand for more precise quantitative forecasting, though the study of the cycle by the leading orthodox neo-classicals hardly got under way in the English-speaking world much before the First World War. The early attempts at trade-cycle forecasting, however, did not usually make much use of the wide variety of theories or models of the cycle then being developed, but rather built up statistics of fluctuations – as did Juglar himself in his great work – more in terms of prices than of incomes and outputs, and tried to predict largely by means of extrapolation. The turning-points of the Juglar cycle were, of course, the key focal points for prediction. Various types of economic barometers were experimented with, mostly in the United States, and mostly in terms of price movements, and as a service more for private business and investors than for the guidance of government policies.

Bertrand de Jouvenel has written of the aloof 'Olympian detachment' of neo-classical theorising from mundane problems of prediction which was only broken down with the advent of Keynesian and national-income theories and policies in the last thirty years.[9] More recently – and perhaps the early sixties may, in Britain, appear as something of a turning-point – the demand and supply of predictions, short-term and long-term, throughout the main divisions of economic theory and policy, has surged up, branching out into such 'exogenous' adjacent socio-economic and social areas as scientific manpower, and young people qualified for University places in 1985 or 2000.

The very marked increase in the demand for economists by business and government, in Britain at any rate, in the last decade, has been very largely, or almost entirely, a demand for predictions. The huge upsurge in the demand for predictions, more frequent predictions, and more accurate predictions, which has come from business and government, has behind it both the much lengthier complexity and 'roundaboutness' of contemporary technology, and the demands of the electorate for more successful policies, perhaps sometimes for quite Utopian levels of performance in terms of a wider and wider range of objectives or *desiderata*. The older classical and neo-classical qualitative predictive judgments could not meet these heightened policy-requirements. Predictions must now be predominantly quantitative and this is what economists and econometricians seek to supply. Increasing quantification has in turn meant that economists in their criteria, objectives, and methods, have attempted to follow much more closely and explicitly the natural sciences. In fact, some economists and econometricians have attempted to define or describe more precisely the kind of predictions they were claiming to produce as 'scientific', in the same sense as the predictions of the most advanced natural sciences. We must now briefly consider the kind of qualities in predictions which have been held to merit this rather overworked adjective.

III

A clear definition of 'scientific prediction' has been set out by Sir Karl Popper in his account of causal explanations and predictions, and is to the effect that an explanation or prediction should be accepted as 'scientific' if, *and only if*, it is deduced from a universal law that has been well tested and corroborated, and from specific initial conditions which have been independently checked. For phenomena to be susceptible to scientific prediction, they must, according to Popper, be 'well-isolated, stationary and recurrent'.[10] But it seems that unless one interprets this standard so loosely as almost or completely to abandon any standard at all, it must be recognised that, so far, in economics and the social sciences, virtually no, or very few, predictively significant, non-trivial laws, or generalisations, have been discovered, which meet up, even approximately, to such a standard.[11]

If it were argued, for example, that the law of demand is such a sufficiently precise and well-tested law or generalisation (and this is certainly one of the less unsatisfactory candidates for the title) then one must insist that the accompanying component, essential for predictive purposes, of checkable and predictable specific initial conditions – regarding tastes, incomes and other prices – has until now, not been adequately available.[12]

Of course, 'scientific laws' in economics, on which useful scientific predictions can be based in this strict and precise 'natural scientific' or 'physico-chemical' sense, conceivably may or might exist. There *may* one day be convincing evidence of the existence of some really significant examples. But usually, neither of the two conditions, or two facets of one condition (satisfactory laws and initial conditions), on which their existence would depend, is present, and if, or when, one of them is, it is nullified by the absence of the other.

Of course, it can reasonably be argued that the differences

between strict 'physico-chemical' predictions in this sense, and what has so far been achieved in the way of economic and social predictions, are simply a matter of degree. Physicists cannot predict the fall of a leaf, or the precise results of a fire or a thunderstorm. A scientific prediction cannot of course, in any specific case, be *absolutely* certain. There may have been a mistake in the checking of the initial conditions, and even an extremely well-tested and corroborated general law might eventually one day be abandoned in the face of new evidence. But the degree of precision and testing of both components is surely of quite a different order of magnitude, and the magnitude of this difference of degree is surely crucial, both in terms of the practical policy-uses of predictions, and in terms of intellectual realism.

The difficulty of putting up any reasonably clear definition of what can be meant by 'scientific prediction' in economics, if one does not use what we are calling the precise 'natural-scientific' or 'physico-chemical' concept, can be illustrated by the attempt made by Professor Theil at the start of his major treatise on *Economic Forecasts and Policy*. Professor Theil does not mention any such criterion as that which we have been discussing, that is, that of being based on a well-tested law, perhaps because he realises that it would set him unattainable standards. But he tries to lay down the requirements which predictions should meet if they are to merit what he calls 'the weighty adjective scientific'. He simply says that they must at least be verifiable and unambiguous as regards the concepts and timing they contain, though, of course, however verifiable (or falsifiable) and *un*ambiguous a prediction may be, it may still merely be, as Theil says, 'the result of the forecaster's imagination'. As Professor Theil goes on:

> It is not easy and even not fruitful to generalise about this point but this at least can be said: the forecasting procedure must be based on theoretical considerations – however simple – and on empirical observations obtained beforehand – however scanty and crude.

Professor Theil's discussion seems to amount to conceding that there is no useful significant definition or criterion of 'scientific' prediction in economics or econometrics.[13]

But if no significant criterion of 'scientific prediction' in economics and econometrics has been produced that will stand up, then an impressive air of strenuous scientific rigour may sometimes be fostered by wrapping up guesses and estimates in complex sets of equations. As Dr. E. F. Schumacher has complained:

> To produce figures about the unknown, the current method is to make a guess about something or other – called an 'assumption' – and to derive an estimate from it by subtle calculation. The estimate is then presented as the result of '*scientific*' reasoning, something *far* superior to mere guesswork. . . The study here under review employs a vast array of arbitrary assumptions, which are then, as it were, put into a calculating machine to produce a '*scientific*' result. It would have been cheaper, and indeed more honest, simply to assume the result.[14]

It seems sometimes to be imagined, that is, that a set of guesses, few if any of which will stand up on their own as in any sense 'scientific predictions', can somehow prop one another up like a house of cards. Scientific status or reliability gets equated with sheer complexity or ingenuity. If it has to be admitted that the actual resulting predictions are often not demonstrably more accurate than what would be achieved by less complex or pretentious methods, the promise is repeatedly held out of predictive triumphs just round the next corner from some new and still more elaborate model or from the latest fashionable revisions and refinements.

On the subject of excessive claims for a kind of natural-scientific prediction and predictability in economics we would like to examine briefly an example from Professor Lipsey's widely influential *Introduction to Positive Economics*. Discussing the nature of what he calls 'scientific prediction' Professor Lipsey writes:

A theory enables us to predict as yet unobserved events. What is the nature of a *scientific prediction*, and is it the same thing as being able to *prophesy the future* course of events? The critical thing to notice about a scientific prediction is that it is a conditional statement of the form: *if* you do this *then* such and such will follow. *If* you mix hydrogen and oxygen under specified conditions, *then* water will be the result. *If* the government has a large budget deficit, *then* the volume of employment will be increased.[15]

Two comments should be made here. *First*, we meet – as one so often does in discussions of prediction in economics – this adjective 'scientific' or the concept of '*scientific prediction*', and we are told here that the critical thing to notice about a 'scientific prediction' is that it is conditional. On the contrary, simply to tell us that a 'scientific' prediction is a conditional statement, gets us almost nowhere. The point is not necessarily invalid, though it is not always and inevitably quite correct – as in astronomy and meteorology. But it is hardly even *a* critical point, much less *the* critical point – rather an *un*critical point. It is barely necessary and it does not begin to be sufficient. The *critical* point about 'scientific' predictions is *the kind of generalisations on which they are based, and whether this is, or should be, a well-tested law.* Anyhow, conditional predictions are more or less useless unless the conditions themselves can be controlled or predicted.

The *second* comment or question relates to the justification for putting side by side the chemical prediction regarding hydrogen, oxygen and water, and the economic prediction regarding a budget deficit and the level of employment, as though these two conditional predictions were reasonably similar in precision and applicability. (Presumably Professor Lipsey carefully chose *a*, or *the* example from macro-economics which would demonstrate his point to the best advantage.) But the chemical prediction is relatively precise, quantitatively and temporally, and it is deduced from a precise and repeatedly well-tested generalisation or law, and from easily testable specific initial conditions (which, in fact, are probably being replicated and confirmed in school laboratories on most days in the year). The economic prediction, on the contrary, starts from a pretty imprecise generalisation – about budget deficits and the level of employment which, as Profesor Lipsey is aware, to be tested would have to be made precise without being turned into a tautology. Presumably this generalisation is *not* simply saying that if there is a net addition there is more. Also, it depends on initial conditions which are not set out with precision, and are far from being anything like as easily and precisely checkable as those of the chemical prediction. Presumably some sort of *ceteris paribus* assumption is being used which it may be impossible to check accurately. Quantitatively and temporally it is highly imprecise. *How* large is a *large* budget deficit, and just *when*, after a week, a month, or a year, will the increase in employment occur?

This economic generalisation however is certainly not useless. Far from it. In the last 25 years vast policy changes have ultimately been based upon it. Epistemologically it is, indeed, a representative example of the sort of theoretical material which the economic forecaster has to use as artfully as he can. It can play a part, if adequately precise and up-to-date statistics are available, in assisting towards less *in*accurate predictions, sometimes requiring some luck for success, and nearly always requiring some, or much, art or judgment. It is, however, highly dangerous to suggest to a beginner student, by juxtaposing these two generalisations – the chemical and the economic – that he will be dealing in economics with generalisations that are comparable, scientifically, epistemologically, and for predictive purpose, with a basic law of chemistry.

IV

Since very few or no fully adequate 'scientific' laws, in the physico-chemical or natural-scientific sense, have been established in economics, on which economists can base predictions,

what are used, *and have to be used*, for predictive purposes
are *trends, tendencies, or patterns*, expressed in empirical or
historical generalisations of less than universal validity, restricted by local and temporal limits. However, Sir Karl Popper
has drawn a sharp and fundamental distinction between laws
and trends and has sternly warned against the use of trends
for predictive purposes:

> Trends exist, or more precisely, the assumption of trends is
> often a useful statistical device. *But trends are not laws.* A
> statement asserting the existence of a trend is existential, not
> universal... The practical significance of this logical
> situation is considerable: while we may base scientific
> predictions on laws, we cannot (as every cautious statistician
> knows) base them merely on the existence of trends. A trend
> (we may again take population growth as an example) which
> has persisted for hundreds or even thousands of years may
> change within a decade, or even more rapidly than that.
>   It is important to point out that *laws and trends are
> radically different things.*[16]

Sir Karl's criticism was directed especially against 'historicist
prophecies', or unconditional predictions based on large-scale
and long-term trends, like the 'prophecies' of Hegel and
Marx. But of course, predictions could be based on trends without being unconditional, large-scale, or long-term. Nor need a
'trend' or 'tendency' represent some changing or 'dynamic'
process. To take Sir Karl's example, a constant population over
a certain period would represent a kind of trend as much as
one growing at a particular rate over the same period. It is
certainly highly desirable to emphasise the seriousness of the
error of treating trends and tendencies as laws. As Sir Karl
maintains, the 'confusion of laws with trends is indefensible',
and this confusion has all too often, over the decades and
centuries, been indulged in by economists. But Sir Karl goes on
to insist: 'A trend, as opposed to a law, must not in general be
used as a basis for scientific predictions.'[17]

Unfortunately this pronouncement seems to rule out 'scientific predictions' in economics. *In fact economists have constantly used, and are constantly using, trends, tendencies, patterns or temporary constancies, as the basis for predictions, because, in fact, they have not available any genuine, relevant, non-trivial laws.* This does not mean that economists' predictions are, or need be, pretentiously 'historicist', in the sense of being unconditional, long-term, or large-scale (of which defects the two latter seem not to be precisely definable).

For an example of an economic prediction based not on a law but on a trend or temporary constancy we may again turn to Professor Lipsey who proposed that we can predict 'with a high degree of confidence' on the basis of what amounts to a constant trend, or tendency, when he proposes that:

> If all the measures of the elasticity of demand [for herrings], over a period of 20 years lay between 1.2 and 1.45, then we would predict the effects of various changes in the herring market with a close degree of accuracy and a high degree of confidence.[18]

Professor Lipsey here is certainly describing how economists *in fact do try* to base their predictions, and how in the nature of the case they *have* to base their predictions, *if* they are predicting at all: that is, they have to do so on the basis of a trend or tendency, the evidence for which is often much slighter than that afforded by twenty years of reliable and tidy observations. Their detailed predictions, that is, are often, or usually, on the basis of some kind of historical series. In fact, predictions derived from economic or econometric models are usually historically based predictions on the basis of *trends*, or on the basis of 'assumptions' derived from trends. For a series of observations about elasticities of demand, confined to twenty years in a single market, could only logically represent a trend or tendency, not a law. It surely cannot be claimed to be a universal law, that in all markets, in all countries, at all times, the elasticity of demand for herrings is, and has always been, between 1.2 and 1.45, and it surely cannot be insisted that it is in *any* sense '*impossible*' that it should be outside those limits.

Similarly *Pareto*'s law, quite obviously, and *Engel*'s law, clearly should be regarded as *trends* and not *laws*. It may be that law-like status can be claimed for the law of diminishing returns, or variable proportions. But our argument is not basically concerned with how, precisely, the law of variable proportions, or Engel's law, or other such marginal cases, are to be interpreted, or with just how broadly or strictly one is to intepret the concept of a well-tested and corroborated scientific law and its specific initial conditions. The obvious fact is that the vast majority of economic predictions are not now and *cannot* now be based on any such laws, but on *trends*. If, then, trends inevitably play such a basic role in all economic, econo-metric or social prediction, then they must be searched for as such. *Of course*, trends are not as reliable as strict, natural-scientific, physico-chemical laws:[19] they, or their interpreta-tions, are often wide open to every kind of subjective ideological bias. But, at the moment, at any rate, they are all, or virtually all, on which economists and econometricians *can* base the kind of significant predictions and forecasts which are being in-creasingly demanded and which will certainly in one form or other get supplied.[20]

We must certainly agree with Sir Karl Popper that the dis-tinction between laws and trends is not only fundamental epistemologically but has great practical significance. If, as economists have so often in the past seemed to be claiming, they had discovered 'Laws', *accompanied by precise, checkable initial conditions*, then they would have been dealing with very high probabilities, or *virtual* certainties, and economic pre-diction would consist largely or entirely of *deduction*, or of logical, mathematical or geometrical *calculation*, as in the kind of textbook or blackboard exercises which comprise so much of elementary economics. On the other hand, to recognise that the main fruit-bearing contribution of economists to policy-making must inevitably come from *trend-spotting*, not by deduction from laws, is to recognise that the task is essentially one of the exercising of *judgment* in a world of uncertainty and ignorance. Moreover, a definition of a 'trend', 'tendency', or 'pattern' must be more arbitrary than most definitions, in particular regarding what should, or should not, be included or excluded in terms of the nature and length of the sequence. Nor does it seem that probabilities can be estimated or applied significantly in this area. There would appear to be some obvious implications for the training of economists directed towards real-world usefulness which we shall mention later.

There is a further methodological lesson which seems to tell against an excessive or exclusivist pro-deductive, and anti-inductive approach. Rather platitudinous observations are constantly repeated about how one cannot collect facts without a prior principle of selection and a terminology in which to describe them; and that heaps of facts do not, of course, of their own accord, arrange themselves significantly. But if forecasting or predicting in economics inevitably depends on the judicious extrapolation of trends, induction seems to be much more centrally involved than the hypothetical-deductivist methodology allows (distilled as it has been mainly from the history of the more 'advanced' natural sciences). Extrapolation of trends by a kind of induction is a method which has obvious weaknesses. But beggars can't be choosers, and if, in some important branches of economic prediction, inductive extrapolation is an inevitable or demonstrably superior method, *because of the nature of the material*, then it must be recognised, and the best must be made of it; and, in fact *quite naive* inductivist extrapolation *has been shown* in some cases in economics to score roughly as well as, or better than, in terms of predictive batting averages, the most elaborate, 'rigorous' deductive model-building.

V

To deny that anything or much in the form of economic laws has been discovered as a basis for relevant 'scientific' predictions, in the natural-scientific sense, certainly implies a high degree of scepticism regarding some of the claims about laws and their predictive potential which economists at various times have asserted or suggested. But such scepticism does not imply that economists cannot and should not attempt to improve on pre-scientific or common-sense predictions by using trends, tendencies or patterns. In fact it can hardly be doubted that over the last two centuries economists have achieved in many directions a very gradual but quite significant improvement in predictive 'batting averages' (as Samuelson calls them). It is important to grasp what the main factor in this improvement has been.

Of course it is dangerous to generalise without a detailed survey of predictive performances and methods throughout as wide a range as possible of the various kinds of economic, econometric and social predictions. No very hard evidence is available to test big, vague, imprecise generalisations to the effect that predictions are generally improving in accuracy, or that economists predict less inaccurately than non-economists – however precisely one draws the dividing line between these two categories. It can, however, reasonably be argued that taking a very long-term view, over the decades, or over a century or two, *on the average*, standards of prediction and forecasting have presumably *very gradually* improved, and *might* reasonably be expected, within limits, to continue *very gradually* to improve.

Let us take briefly, as rough indications, the basic *long*-run prediction of population, on the one hand, and the basic *short*-run prediction of GNP on the other hand. Even the most expert population predictions, as those of the British Royal Commission of 1949, and even of Government Committees after that date, not to mention some of the predictions in the thirties, and those on which the Beveridge Report was based, had, within a decade or two, gone quite seriously wrong by magnitudes of up to 20 per cent or more. But such errors pale into insignificance if one considers that about 250 years ago a leading thinker or authority of his day like Montesquieu –

as Bertrand de Jouvenel has pointed out – could go so wildly astray as to proclaim that world population was in the process of a steep decline. Similarly Rousseau could proclaim, 200 years ago, that the population of England was in the process of falling heavily. It would be difficult to predict quite so completely wrongly, both with regard to magnitude and to direction, today.[21]

It is perfectly obvious, and methodologically significant, what the main primary factor responsible in the last two hundred years for the diminution in *in*accuracy has been. Montesquieu and Rousseau had no accurate statistics of what the population was, or what it had been 10, 50 or 100 years previously. Unquestionably the first thing to do in order to diminish the inaccuracy of forecasts of what the population is going to be 10, 50 or 100 years from now, is to get as recent and accurate figures as possible of what it is now, or rather has been in recent decades.

Similarly, until about the nineteen-forties in this country, one could hardly achieve that measure of accuracy in predicting next year's GNP, or next year's unemployment percentage, which could subsequently be attained, vastly inadequate though this still was for the achievement of the *much* higher policy ambitions which had come to be held. This was primarily because there were then no regularly and systematically collected recent and accurate figures of national income – the emergence of which was the main constructive scientific consequence of what is called 'the Keynesian revolution', and in which, of course, there is still much room for more accuracy and up-to-dateness. Of course, also, there have been the analytical questions to sort out regarding the definition and components of GNP, and even, to a much lesser extent, regarding population.

So long as the statistics of what you are trying to predict are getting more accurate and more up-to-date, one prime, necessary, though needless to say, far from sufficient condition for making less inaccurate social and economic predictions is being satisfied. This, therefore, could be said to be the *first* and main factor in achieving improved economic predictions. Though unable to feel complete confidence in the present Director's hope and belief that the National Institute of Economic and Social Research will be forecasting 'better' a hundred years hence, we certainly agree with him as to what will most probably turn out to have been the reason for any improvement, *if* it has occurred:

> I am prepared to believe, and certainly hope, that the National Institute forecasts a hundred years hence will be better than they are today; but I suspect that my successor will be saying that the main improvement comes from knowing more accurately where the economy actually is, because his data are more accurate and up-to-date than the ones we have today.[22]

What might be considered the other two main factors in achieving more accurate predictions are, *secondly*, an improved model or formal theoretical component; and *thirdly*, an improved informal, *ad hoc* or inexplicit, theoretical component, based on improved hunch and judgment either in supplementing, applying and adapting, formal theories or models, or in the use of interpretation of the available statistics. Of course these three factors are not independent. The ultimate ideal aim must include a valid model. But the best feasible approach, while this ideal is out of reach, may be improvements in judgment and in statistical material.

As regards (2), the models and formal theoretical components, great hopes and perhaps a vastly excessive concentration of effort have been devoted to striving for improvements by means of sheer elaboration and complexity – as though this was the essential prime means by which predictions were to be formulated or improved regardless of the quality of the basic material. As a leading authority some time ago maintained (and there do not seem to have been any highly significant changes in the meantime):

> We must face the fact that models using elaborate theoretical

and statistical tools and concepts have not done decisively better, in the majority of available tests, than the most simple-minded and mechanical extrapolation formulae.[23]

As regards the *third* factor, hunch or judgment, or the informal, unsystematised ability to spot trends and their turning-points, a recent survey of the forecasting of the UK economy by the Treasury puts most weight on this factor if improved economic predictions are to be achieved:

Inasmuch as it appears that most forecasting error is attributable to non-systematic factors, it may well be that an essential prerequisite for improved economic forecasting is further refinement in the traditional judgment of the forecasters themselves.[24]

Much education in economics does little or nothing to cultivate, and may indeed worsen, the 'refinement in the traditional judgment' of economists, which is rightly recognised here as having such an essential role in the fruitful application of economic knowledge. In fact, the key role of judgment seems often not to have even been recognised; or it is assumed that the need for judgment is unfortunate but temporary and that it will soon be largely eliminated by the progress of science. Judgment may, indeed, be far more difficult to cultivate, teach and inculcate, than technical calculation and analysis.

VI

Although we have been concerned to emphasise the hardly questionable improvement, over the last two hundred years, of economists' ability to predict many or most – though not all – kinds of economic behaviour, we also remarked that we were unable to share the kind of unqualified official optimism (earlier expressed by the Director of the NIESR) that this improving trend will certainly, or highly probably, continue over

the next hundred years. The very gradual improvement *may*
continue: but we must examine, in conclusion, some reasons
for supposing that it may not. Unqualified official optimism
should be accepted with some reserve. For example, in a lecture
of 1964 the Economic Adviser to HMG was expressing considerable confidence regarding improved prediction of the most
important factors in short-run economic management:

> We are enormously further on than twenty-five years ago:
> and if we take enough trouble in the next twenty-five years
> we may make just as much progress in improving our
> understanding of the functioning of the economic system
> and our power to forecast its behaviour.[25]

Much progress between 1939 and 1964 can hardly be denied,
though just *how* much is very difficult to assess. But can this
progress simply be extrapolated on to 1989 and through the
twenty-first century? A recent detailed study of the record of
the decade or so down to 1971 concludes:

> There is no evidence of any improvements in predictive
> accuracy over time of either the Treasury or National
> Institute forecasts, nor that the proportion of systematic
> error has been reduced.

Certainly it is conceded:

> The forecasters usually earn their keep in that their pre-
> dictions tend to be more accurate than those generated by
> naive models.[26]

We certainly would not claim that there is, so far, any very
significant weight of evidence that either (a) economic predictions are generally declining in accuracy; or (b) that the
economy, or economic behaviour in general, is becoming more
difficult to predict. Nor, of course, are we suggesting that some
kind of technical or intellectual decline is setting in, or about
to set in, among economic forecasters. But batsmen's averages

might fall significantly, even though their skill and application were definitely improving, if the bowling was getting more difficult or the pitches were deteriorating.

Moreover, while the capacity to predict less inaccurately might still be improving, the range and standard of accuracy demanded by policy ambitions may well rise at least in proportion. Basically, it may be intellectually healthy for the pressure of policy demand always to be pressing on the supply of economic knowledge, or predictive capacity. However, the danger always exists – quite apart from the disappointment of expectations – that policy performance may be even worse than it might have been, because the supply of less inaccurate predictions is not technically forthcoming to meet policy demands for higher and higher levels of achievement over a wider and wider range of policy objectives. There are obviously special dangers if these over-ambitious demands are actually stimulated by naive intellectual pretensions on the supply side as when would-be advisers seek influence with politicians.

But it is not only that even if the economists' supply of predictions were to continue gradually to improve in quantity and quality, they will continue to appear inadequate, and perhaps increasingly inadequate, relative to an increasingly urgent and extravagant demand. There is a further possibility to be faced, which must qualify any tendency to optimism, and which is deeper and more serious, though more imprecise, speculative and uncertain. Although the instruments and techniques of prediction may be improving, this might be counterbalanced, or more than counterbalanced, by the fact that some economic phenomena were becoming more difficult to predict, so that the economist's task was indeed a Sisyphean one. That is, there may be significant currents of increasing unpredictability gathering strength in the economic and social world. This is, of course, a prospect or possibility which the more 'mature' natural sciences do not have to face in the same form. Possibly, also, even the interventions of the economists themselves make their material more difficult to predict.

Let us try to indicate more specifically one or two of the

factors which might be making for a heightened unpredictability of economic and social phenomena. Less than a decade
ago such considerations as these seemed highly speculative.
Now these factors look much more like definite forces to be
reckoned with, which must qualify any optimism about forecasting possibilities, even if they are still difficult to demonstrate conclusively by hard evidence.

I It seems to be widely assumed – though the proposition may
be difficult to test or measure precisely – that the pace of technological change is increasing; and this may well continue even
if the rate of growth were to decline markedly. If so, this will
probably be making the economic and social world in various
ways *more* difficult to predict. The growth of new knowledge
must, to a large extent, be unpredictable, or difficult to predict,
as well as its technological and hence economic consequences.
One need only cite the example of fuel and energy predictions
– in Britain at any rate – which have repeatedly and seriously
gone astray over the last twenty-five years.

II Secondly, it would seem that as living standards have risen,
at least in terms of conventional measurements, the economic
behaviour of the materially more 'affluent' becomes more
difficult to predict with regard to their patterns of consumption
demand and their supply of work. There is a significantly
wider margin, in the long term and in the short term, of 'discretionary' spending or saving, and for the 'discretionary'
supply or withholding of labour on the part of a larger percentage of the population. Economic activity was presumably
more predictable when much, or most, of it – as perhaps
justifiably assumed by the English classicals – was at, or much
nearer, the margin of subsistence than it is in the more 'developed' countries today. On the other hand, even in the poorer
countries, where much or most economic behaviour must be
much more closely related to a subsistence margin, outside
disturbances from fundamental technological change and social
upheaval must *tend* to make economic prediction more difficult

than, say, half a century ago. Furthermore, one might generally conclude that in many areas of conduct related to, or affecting, economic processes, patterns of traditional and customary behaviour, whether related or not to subsistence standards, set limits on unpredictability which are now being replaced by waves of fashion which are much more difficult to predict.[27]

III Thirdly, there would appear to have been increasingly important kinds of degrees of *interdependence*, making economic prediction more difficult, (a) in regard to market behaviour; and (b) as between economic and social factors.

(a) Classical and neo-classical economists recognised, and in some cases emphasised, that the conclusions or predictions they reached depended, to a large extent, on the assumption of competitive conditions. Indeed, J. S. Mill proclaimed:

> Only through the principle of competition has political economy any pretension to the character of a science.[28]

Certainly neo-classical theory had far superior equipment for dealing with problems of monopoly than had the classicals. But Edgeworth recognised the difficulties of deriving predictions from 'orthodox' theorising, where oligopolistic, or interacting, processes were involved, which he included under the heading of 'monopoly'. In a regime of monopolies or oligopolies economic 'theory', as understood by Edgeworth, would have largely to abdicate:

> Among those who would suffer by the new regime, there would be one class ... namely the abstract economists, who would be deprived of their occupation, the investigation of the conditions which determine value. There would survive only the empirical school, flourishing in a chaos congenial to their mentality.[29]

Edgeworth may or may not have been justified regarding the occupational prospects of 'abstract economists'. But the point he was making certainly has some relevance to economic developments in the second half of the twentieth century: micro-economic predictions based on standard price theory may well have become more difficult and uncertain, as a possible result of greater 'instability' consequent on the widespread super-session of competitive conditions by various forms of oligopoly and monopoly, in the way adumbrated by Edgeworth.

(b) With regard to social and economic interdependence, rapid technological changes make for social upheavals which react back, largely unpredictably, so far as the economist is concerned, on economic behaviour (as, for example, *via* such phenomena as chronic inflation and 'stagflation'). Economics as a separate discipline developed in its formative classical or neo-classical phases, especially in nineteenth-century Britain, under the broad assumption, which was then fleetingly less unjustifiable, perhaps, than at most other periods in modern history, of a given, stable social framework, or 'stable general culture' as Pigou called it half a century ago. Changes in this social framework in so far as they affected economic processes, might be assumed to be gradual and themselves fairly pre-dictable. Historical, Comteist, Marxist, and Institutionalist economists (who, until recently, never made much headway in the once politically more stable Britain) have always rejected this simplifying assumption, which was, however, more or less essential for most of the kinds of qualitative predictive judg-ments which the orthodox version of the subject was able to contribute.[30]

In confronting and recognising such possibly serious diffi-culties looming over the future of economists' predictive per-formance and capacity, we are simply meeting up again with an aspect of the fundamental differences between economics and the more 'developed' natural sciences. Because of con-stancies in their basic materials, predictive capacity, once attained, regarding many physical or chemical phenomena, can be preserved, added to and accumulated to an extent signifi-cantly beyond what is possible in the social sciences. In eco-nomics and the social sciences it might well be that painfully and fleetingly achieved predictions and predictive capacity may not only lose practical relevance but may break down and even become more difficult to replace, because the basic material might be becoming more difficult, or impossible to predict.

However, we are certainly not, in conclusion, going to attempt to predict the future of economic prediction. We would simply warn against a facile assumption, based on a false analogy with natural sciences, that with regard to predictive performance the only possible direction, at however gradual a pace, is forwards; and that deterioration and less accuracy, without any decline in competence and technique, are out of the question. We would point out, also, the implications for the education or training of economists and forecasters. It has been stated that:

> As economic knowledge grows the area within which it is necessary to apply judgment to forecasts will tend to contract.[31]

Not necessarily so, and perhaps, or even probably, not actually so. The hope that the need to apply judgment will disappear is based on a too static and natural-scientific conception of the task of prediction in economics and the social sciences. The role of judgment, as contrasted with deduction or calculation, far from contracting or fading away with the refinements of 'model'-building, or even with (what is far more important) more accurate and up-to-date statistics, *may* perhaps be about to grow significantly in importance. Cultivating, or educating for judgment may be more difficult than putting students through mathematical and geometrical exercises. But for the economic forecaster the close study of history and historical episodes may have a relatively much more important part to play than training in deductive or mathematical agility. History may inculcate *some* broad grasp of what to expect and what not to expect (as in politics) which is hardly assisted by the endless refinement of the properties of maxima and optima or of peculiarities and *curiosa* suggested by purely logical or taxonomic analysis.

Three
On the History and Philosophy of Science and Economics

I

Methodological questions in economics have often been discussed in terms that are too abstract and too exclusively normative. Slim volumes, or essays, about the 'scope and method' or the 'nature and significance' of the subject, seem often to have been concerned mainly with ideal epistemological models which are almost as remote from the actuality of what economists do, as economic models of smoothly and ideally self-equilibrating processes are remote from the processes of the real economic world.[1] Intellectual norms are prescribed, and, it seems to be implied, are actually upheld, which are certainly not in fact followed and perhaps could not practically *be* followed, by economists.[2] Moreover, generalisations, normative or positive, are inevitably highly abstract, or stylised, when they relate to 'science' and 'scientific method' in general, or to 'the social sciences' generally, or even to economics as a whole, which comprises theories and arguments of very varying epistemological types and calibres.

It could, therefore, constitute a most welcome and significant example, as far as economics is concerned, that in their different ways, in the work of both Kuhn and Lakatos, the history of science, and its analysis or philosophy, have been brought together for mutual illumination. Certainly there is the danger here of normative–positive confusion, in so far as the philosopher of science may be seeking to prescribe what scientists *ought* to have done or decided (or be doing or deciding) while the historian is attempting rather to set out what they actually *did* do or decide.[3] Certainly also one feels bound to record the impression that what economists actually do and decide (and have done and decided) is not, and has not been, invariably what, according to tenable methodological or scientific criteria, they *ought* to have done or decided. Nevertheless, though this danger of normative–positive confusion needs close attention, there does not seem to be any inevitable, fundamental difficulty, ruling out from the start, useful, mutual illumination between the philosophy and the history of economics.

It may well seem, however, that a larger relative component of recent or contemporary history might be more suitable than the relatively heavy concentration on the history of physics from the sixteenth to the early twentieth centuries – which is what 'the history of science' seems to a large extent, though not exclusively, to consist of. Indeed, a relatively greater emphasis on the recent or contemporary history of sciences might seem to be justified, if the estimate is accepted that about 90 per cent or more of the scientists (including presumably physicists and economists) who have ever lived, are alive today.[4]

But we come now to what seems a more serious danger, which is that of drawing methodological lessons, or conclusions, about the development of a wide range of sciences, from a version of the history of science in general which is concentrated too exclusively on a particular kind of success story, that of the development of physics, and similar subjects, from the sixteenth century onwards. In fact, a possibly serious danger which might emanate from the 'history of science', as it seems widely to be pursued, is that of a kind of oversimplified *historicism* of science leading to excessive and misleading generalisations about how sciences *must* develop. There seems to be a danger of forgetting that, as Kuhn puts it, 'the sciences are not, in fact, all of a piece';[5] or that as Ravetz has emphasised:

The world of science is a very variegated one ... and the 'methods' of science are a very heterogeneous collection of things.[6]

The 'history of science', in fact, is not actually made up of a single, epistemologically homogeneous activity, because, basically the nature of the *materials* which different sciences deal with is significantly different. Of course, it is time and again asserted that these differences are only differences of degree, and not of kind or principle. But an insistence on this way of putting it can be seriously misleading when the differences are as wide and consequential as they are. As has been well said:

The single most important discovery of social science in these last decades is that social science does not yield the kind of knowledge of society – and the kind of power over society – that natural science possesses vis-à-vis the natural world.[7]

To some extent, philosophers of science have been recognising differences between sciences simply by distinguishing between what they call 'mature' and 'immature' sciences. This pair of adjectives, as we shall see, has been used by Kuhn, Lakatos and Ravetz, among others, and suggests, rather obviously, the kind of historicism of science which is open to complaint.

If one calls a science 'immature' one seems to be suggesting that *either*, in due course, it will, more or less inevitably, by some natural process of 'maturation' become like physics – the supremely 'mature' science – *or*, if this does not happen, or doesn't seem to be happening, there must be something wrong: the subject is being mishandled and the wrong can be set right by following certain philosophical or methodological prescriptions. It seems even to be suggested that possibly there are inevitable 'stages of development' – to introduce a favourite historicist concept – which must and will be passed through in the development of sciences, as in the development of economies.[8]

Similarly, it is sometimes suggested, in a plausibly optimistic manner, by economists and social scientists, that their subjects got started later, and were left behind by the natural sciences, with the implication that they will, in due course, catch up. But the question has to be posed as to *why* economics and the social sciences somehow started late, or got left behind, if it was not for reasons in the nature of the basic material which may preclude any eventual 'catching up' with physics, or anything like it.

Suggestions of a kind of historicism of science, and of laws, or stages, of development, fail to take account of fundamental differences in material: notably, for example, that the material of physics possesses constancies, and an absence of significant historical change and development, which the material of economics does *not* possess. If the material which economics deals with was to come to resemble, sufficiently significantly, the material which physics deals with, then the science of economics might come in due course to resemble the science of physics in 'maturity' and 'development'. Meanwhile, the often-quoted dictum of Aristotle remains relevant: 'Our discussion will be adequate if it has as much clearness as the subject-matter admits of.'[9]

We would add that not only 'clearness', but what is reached in the way of conclusions, 'theories', predictions and 'laws' (if any), must depend on what 'the subject-matter' of different sciences 'admits of'.

It is certainly not argued here that there are no relevant and valuable methodological lessons, parallels, and examples, which may be drawn for economics from the history of physics and chemistry. There certainly are such. But there are, also, easily assumed, but fundamentally misleading parallels which may be drawn, including a questionable and perhaps unjustified presumption that economics will eventually, one day, come to a 'maturity' resembling that of physics today.[10]

We shall now explore what some leading philosophers of science have recently had to say about economics as a science – notably Sir Karl Popper, T. S. Kuhn, J. R. Ravetz, and Imre

Lakatos – and we shall comment on one or two brief but significant suggestions, by Lakatos and Ravetz, regarding sciences at different stages of 'maturity' or 'immaturity'. It may be remarked at this point that some economists, and their methodological PRO's, seem to have argued confidently over the merits or demerits, so far as economics is concerned, of the methodological analyses and prescriptions of Popper, Kuhn, and Lakatos, without taking into account that the analyses and prescriptions of these distinguished philosophers of science have been derived and distilled, very largely, or almost exclusively, from the history and philosophy of physics or similar subjects. Thus the suggestion is conveyed (which is, of course, likely to be highly popular with some economists) of a kind of epistemological parity between economics and physics, which will render the methodological analysis, prescriptions, strategy or tactics, derived from the one science, entirely appropriate, almost without qualification or reservation, to the other science.

As regards philosophers of science, they seem, in recent decades, to have been rather reticent regarding the particular, peculiar, methodological position of economics. However, they may be found discussing very sharp contrasts between physics, on the one hand – in the history and method of which they have been primarily interested – and certain other social, or 'human' sciences, or subjects, on the other hand. But economics is usually left out of these comparisons and its epistemological position is left somewhat obscure. Alternatively, it seems to be rather too readily assumed that by cultivating the history and philosophy of physics the road is being cleared, paved, and lit up along which, in due course, economics can and will advance to the 'maturity' of physics even if, perhaps, those economists who apparently have professed that it is already far advanced towards that objective may be a little premature. Moreover, insufficient notice and account is taken of precisely what it is in their material which has helped to make some sciences what is called 'mature', and others so much more 'immature'.

II

Let us start with Sir Karl Popper. Sir Karl has told us in his autobiography:

> The social sciences never had for me the same attraction as the theoretical natural sciences.[11]

In *The Open Society*, Popper wrote of 'the somewhat unsatisfactory state of some of the social sciences.' He maintained that 'much of our "social science" belongs to the Middle Ages'[12] (which, apparently, Sir Karl intended as a pejorative judgment). In fact, according to Sir Karl:

> The social sciences do not as yet seem to have found their Galileo . . . There is very little in the social sciences that resembles the objective and ideal quest for truth which we meet in physics.[13]

Moreover, as Sir Karl has subsequently insisted:

> Compared with physics, sociology and psychology are riddled with fashion and with uncontrolled dogmas. . . The natural sciences are largely free from verbal discussion, while verbalism was, and still is, rampant, in many forms in the social sciences.[14]

We would hold, for our part, that though economics may not be exactly 'riddled' with fashion and uncontrolled dogmas, and though 'verbalism' may not be precisely 'rampant' in the subject, nevertheless these phenomena are not exactly conspicuous by their absence from economics. However, Sir Karl's strictures on the social sciences generally are not applied to economic theory, which, he seems to suggest, occupies a quite exceptional position. In fact, in *The Poverty of Historicism* Sir Karl remarks:

D

The success of mathematical economics shows that one
social science at least has gone through its Newtonian
revolution.[15]

Certainly one might find similar claims suggested by mathematical economists. But the mathematical 'revolution' in
economics has been one mainly (or almost entirely) of *form*,
*with very little or no empirical, testable, predictive content in-
volved*. In accepting as 'Newtonian' a purely, or almost purely,
formal, or notational, 'revolution', Sir Karl seems to have
allowed himself to be taken in by over-optimistic propaganda.
Not only has nothing genuinely describable as 'a Newtonian
revolution' taken place in economics, it is reasonable to suggest
that it is not probable that anything of the sort is going to
occur in the foreseeable future. Anyhow, if economic theory,
mathematically formulated, constitutes such a shining, unique
exception and contrast, compared with the 'medieval', pre-
Galilean condition of the social sciences generally, then surely
such an outstanding post-Newtonian salient would deserve the
closest analysis and appraisal *from philosophers of science*, instead of the neglect it has recently, in the main, received.

In *The Poverty of Historicism* Sir Karl held to a predominantly, not exclusively, 'naturalistic' line regarding the social
sciences, that is, he argued in favour of applying in the social
sciences the criteria and methods of the natural sciences. One
might well have derived from Sir Karl's treatment much confidence that if such monstrous errors as 'historicism', 'verbalism', etc., could be exposed and eliminated, then the social
sciences could and would develop and 'mature' along the lines
on which physics had developed and 'matured'. Certainly, one
cannot but acknowledge the force and cogency of most of Sir
Karl's pro-naturalist arguments, and few concessions need or
should be made to the older anti-naturalist attitudes which he
so convincingly criticised. Certainly also, it is desirable to
attempt the advancement of economics and the social sciences
along 'naturalistic' lines *to the utmost, but limited, extent to
which such advance is feasible or possible*. But what it is just

as essential to emphasise is not only that the advance along these lines, though not negligible, has been so far comparatively limited, but that there are no good grounds for supposing that any *very* great advances of the kind and extent made in physics in the last three or four centuries are *very* likely to ensue in economics. Meanwhile, misleading comparisons between economics and physics and the methods, tactics, and criteria appropriate to the two sciences, neglect vital differences in the nature of the basic materials with which they are engaged. It is ultimately because of the differences in basic materials that 'historicism', 'essentialism', 'verbalism', 'fashion', 'uncontrollable dogmas', and all the other methodological monstrosities, discerned by Sir Karl in the social sciences, are so *much* more difficult, or *almost* impossible, to root out, and will not give way very far to methodological prescriptions however trenchant, although significant improvements in this respect are not impossible to achieve, *if critical standards are constantly upheld, however unpopular this may be.*

Sir Karl's over-optimism regarding the post-Newtonian character of economic theory seems to be illustrated by his claim that sociological or economic laws or hypotheses exist, 'which are analogous to the laws or hypotheses of the natural sciences'. As Sir Karl shows:

Every natural law can be expressed by asserting that *such and such a thing cannot happen*; that is to say, by a sentence in the form of the proverb: 'You can't carry water in a sieve.'[16]

Sir Karl then claims to cite parallel examples of such laws or hypotheses in economics:

'You cannot introduce agricultural tariffs and at the same time reduce the cost of living.' – 'You cannot in an industrial society, organise consumers' pressure groups as effectively as you can organise certain producers' pressure groups.' – 'You cannot have a centrally planned society with a price system that fulfils the main functions of competitive prices.' – 'You cannot have full employment without inflation.'

These generalisations, listed by Sir Karl, are certainly not useless. They represent the kind of rough-and-ready material, in the form of patterns, trends, or tendencies, which economists have to work with if they do not – as some do – take refuge in 'rigorous' fantasies and unrealities. But these generalisations do not really begin to compare with their counterparts in physics in terms of reasonably precise, testable and well-tested, empirical and predictive content. Behind the informal, pro-verbial, physical generalisation about the impossibility of carry-ing water in a sieve, there stand the kind of well-tested laws, with precise measurable and easily tested initial conditions, which one relies on when travelling by aeroplane or crossing a bridge. *Virtually no laws of this quality, or of anything approaching this quality, stand behind Sir Karl's collection of economic generalisations*, which, indeed, simply confirm that:

A typical law in the physical sciences is stated precisely, usually in mathematical terms, and is quite free of ambiguity. It has been tested repeatedly and has withstood the tests. The usual law in the social sciences, on the other hand, is ordinarily couched in Big Words and a great deal of ambiguity.[17]

Admittedly in Sir Karl's economic generalisations he does not descend to 'Big Words', but he does not avoid 'a great deal of ambiguity'. Anyhow, later on in *The Poverty of Histori-cism* Sir Karl agrees that:

It cannot be doubted that *there are some fundamental difficulties here*. In physics, for example, the parameters of our equations can, in principle, be reduced to a small number of natural constants – a reduction which has been successfully carried out in many important cases. This is not so in economics; here the parameters are themselves in the most important cases quickly changing variables. This clearly reduces the significance, interpretability, *and testability* of our measurements.[18]

Unfortunately, Sir Karl broke off at this point without commenting on the significance of these 'fundamental difficulties' for his claims regarding sociological and economic laws, 'analogous to the laws or hypotheses of the natural sciences', and for that 'Newtonian revolution' in economic theory which he had claimed to discern. But if the parameters in economic theories, or quasi-theories, are 'in the most important cases quickly changing variables', and there are no reliable laws, but only historical trends or patterns, on which to base predictions, then the question arises as to the relevance and suitability *for economics* of the strongly anti-inductive emphasis in Popper's methodology. Such methodological principles may have been most serviceable in physics, from the history of which they have been derived. But they may be too exclusivist for a subject with a fundamental historical aspect, like economics. The relevance of methodological principles must depend on the nature of the material with which a particular subject has to deal. It is not good advice to condemn induction if the nature of the material restricts the genuine scope for the hypothetico-deductive method. And the material with which economics has to deal shows certain crucial differences from the material with which physics has to deal, which it is dangerously misleading to neglect. As Professor M. J. Roberts has argued:

As a first step, social scientists must recognise that all science is not physics. Physics has obtained equations that apply to all electrons because all electrons are in the relevant sense alike. When phenomena are heterogenous, generality can only be obtained at the price of content. One is forced to say less and less about each case in order to include all possible cases. Such abstract non-phenomena-orientated theorizing in the social sciences, most emphatically cannot be justified by analogy to basic research in natural science since the latter, unlike the former, is concerned with explicating real empirical events.[19]

However, it is essential to distinguish between Sir Karl's rather over-optimistic, incidental comments on economic theory, which may well have fostered a certain complacency among some economists, and his general prescriptions in terms of a vitally valuable, and salutary, critical 'falsificationism'. We shall return later to the contrasting effects on economists of Sir Karl's teachings.

III

Let us now turn very briefly to T. S. Kuhn's writings, in which there is little or nothing specifically about economics, but which employ the concept of 'mature' and 'immature' sciences (also used, as we shall see, by Ravetz and Lakatos). 'Immature' sciences, or 'proto-sciences' as Kuhn calls them, are those

> in which practice does generate testable conclusions but which nonetheless resemble philosophy and the arts rather than the established sciences in their developmental patterns ... The proto-sciences like the arts and philosophy, lack some element which, in the mature sciences permits the more obvious forms of progress. It is not, however, anything that a methodological prescription can provide.

Kuhn includes 'many of the social sciences today', alongside the arts and philosophy, among the 'proto-sciences', as contrasted with the 'established' or 'mature' sciences.

In view of the way in which Kuhn's earlier views and concepts were unjustifiably exploited and misrepresented – by some economists among others – it may be worth underlining the fairly hard criteria which he sets out for scientific 'maturity'. These criteria include the following:

First is Sir Karl's demarcation criterion without which no field is potentially a science. . . *Second* . . . predictive success must be consistently achieved. . . *Third*, predictive techniques must have roots in a theory. . .[20]

The uncertain position of economics could be indicated by citing the quite contradictory views that leading economists have expressed, and are expressing, regarding just such issues as these three.[21]

It is to be noted that Kuhn agrees regarding Popper's falsificationist prescriptions:

Even in the developed sciences, there is an essential role for Sir Karl's methodology. It is the strategy appropriate to those occasions when something goes wrong with normal science.[22]

It may be suggested that in the 'underdeveloped' science of economics (as the President of the Royal Economic Society has recently called it) or in 'immature' sciences generally, there nearly always is, or has been – from any not thoroughly complacent and uncritical point of view – 'something going wrong'. In other words there hardly ever is, or has been, an even *relatively* adequately based 'normality' in such subjects, comparable with 'normality' in physics. So whether or not one accepts Kuhn's concept of 'normality' for a 'developed' or 'mature' science, such as physics (which is a condition when, according to Kuhn, Sir Karl's strategy or prescriptions would be inappropriate), *a fortiori*, in Kuhn's view, there is *always* a role for those trenchant Popperian prescriptions in economics and the social sciences, contrary to what is maintained by economists and sociologists who have purveyed a false impression of Kuhn's views in order to controvert Popper's.

IV

Let us turn next to a contribution which, though it may not seem to present a fairly balanced appraisal of the state of economics, certainly deserves much more attention from economists, or philosophers of the subject, than it has so far received. This contribution is contained in Dr. J. R. Ravetz's massive work on *Scientific Knowledge and its Social Problems*. Dr. Ravetz provides a much fuller, more explicit and more severe appraisal of where economics belongs in the spectrum of the sciences, than Popper, Kuhn, or Lakatos. Using, like Kuhn, and as we shall see, Lakatos, the terminology of 'mature' and 'immature' subjects, Ravetz places economics firmly among what he calls, in a chapter of that title, 'Immature and Ineffective Fields of Enquiry'. According to Ravetz:

> At the present time, the disciplines that present the most obvious evidence of ineffectiveness or at least immaturity, are those which attempt to study human behaviour in the style of the mathematical-experimental sciences ... The situation becomes worse when an immature or ineffective field is enlisted in the work of resolution of some practical problem.[23]

Somehow Dr. Ravetz seems to have missed Sir Karl's 'Newtonian Revolution' in mathematical economics. He goes on, with reference to economics:

> In spite of the vacuity or irrelevance of most of its theory and the patent unreliability of its statistical information, it ranks as the queen of the sciences in the formation of national policy.[24]

Dr. Ravetz perceives very clearly where the root of the difficulty lies:

The condition of ineffectiveness is not an accidental deficiency in some component of the materials of a field, but is a systematic weakness in those materials.[25]

Next to be emphasised is a distinction which Ravetz draws, which is somewhat similar to one made by Kuhn, and also, as we shall see, by Lakatos. This is, that in subjects of different levels of 'maturity' or 'immaturity', methodological criteria or 'criteria of adequacy', have to be enforced with different degrees of stringency. Ravetz maintains that in a field which has 'achieved maturity', with a 'set of appropriate and stable criteria of adequacy', such methodological criteria

become part of the basic unselfconscious craft knowledge of the field; . . . In these conditions the very existence of criteria of adequacy can be overlooked.[26]

In other words, in thoroughly 'mature' fields, what we shall find Lakatos describing as 'Polanyite autonomy' may be accepted or tolerated as appropriate. *On the other hand, as Ravetz insists, 'in less mature fields', criteria of adequacy or methodological standards 'cannot be taken for granted'.*

Dr. Ravetz points out the problems in terms of funds and prestige of admitting or recognising 'immaturity' in a subject:

The present social institutions of science, and of learning in general, impose such constraints that the growth and even the survival of an immature field would be endangered by the simple honesty of public announcement of its condition. For these institutions were developed around mature or rapidly maturing fields in the nineteenth century. . . If the representatives of a discipline announce that they do not fit in with such a system, they can be simply excluded from it, to the benefit of their competitors for the perennially limited resources. The field would be relegated to amateur status, and thereby pushed over to the very margin of the world of learning; it would be deprived of funds and prestige.[27]

But appearances can be deceptive:

> An immature field, in chaos internally, experiences the
> additional strains of hypertrophy; its leaders and
> practitioners are exposed to the temptations of being accepted
> as consultants and experts for the rapid solution of urgent
> practical problems. The field can soon become identical in
> outward appearance to an established physical technology,
> but in reality be a gigantic confidence-game... To thread
> one's way through these pitfalls, making a genuine
> contribution both to scientific knowledge and to the welfare
> of society, requires a combination of knowledge and
> understanding in so many different areas of experience,
> that its only correct title is wisdom.[28]

Dr. Ravetz concludes:

> Since immature and ineffective fields are due to be involved
> in public affairs to an increasing extent as our social problems
> become ever more complex, an awareness of their limitations
> is necessary if their application is to produce more good than
> harm.[29]

Possibly Dr. Ravetz is excessively censorious and gloomy regarding economics and its potential contribution. In particular,
the heavily value-loaded words 'immature', 'ineffective' and
'weakness' are unnecessary and inappropriate. The state of
economics and the nature of its material are simply *different*
from those of physics. But this kind of critical severity may be
much less dangerous than the excessive optimism and pre-
tentiousness which has been so much more common among
economists. *The dangers which Dr. Ravetz stresses should not
be underestimated.* Surely he is right in maintaining that to
inculcate an awareness of the limitations of the subject is today
a major, and perhaps *the* major, task of the philosopher of
economics, rather than the suggestion of misleading and over-
optimistic parallels between economics and physics. The limita-

tions of economic knowledge and its 'ineffectiveness' are not to any *very* large extent the fault of economists. There is no simple methodological remedy or formula for 'maturity' and 'effectiveness'. A reallocation of economists' efforts, or a re-shaping of their education and training, might be both illumi-nating and marginally beneficial in terms of less unsuccessful policy-making, but could hardly provide solutions satisfying the excessive expectations which have grown up regarding government policies. However, failure to grasp limitations and a failure to try to bring them home to politicians and public, could certainly constitute a *very* serious fault, as would still more so, the fostering of excessive expectations.

V

Imre Lakatos also – like Kuhn and Ravetz – employed the distinction between 'mature sciences' and what he called 'im-mature and indeed dubious disciplines'. (Incidentally it might be useful to pinpoint *exactly* what it is in this context that is 'dubious' and why.) Lakatos also referred to 'the under-developed social sciences', and to 'a process of degeneration' occurring in 'some of the main schools of modern sociology, psychology and social psychology.'[30]

But the only explicit reference to economics to be found in his writings claimed that:

> The reluctance of economists and other social scientists to accept Popper's methodology may have been partly due to the destructive effects of naive falsificationism on budding research programmes.[31]

We shall return later to the alleged 'reluctance' of economists 'to accept Popper's methodology' (which reluctance became indeed considerable, but far from total, and may have been based on widely differing and contrasting grounds). Anyhow, presumably the reluctance of economists, or of anyone else, to

accept what is 'naive' and (unduly) 'destructive' *must* be justified. One may well agree that it provides, in some ways, a more
enlightening historical perspective to look at 'research programmes' rather than particular theories or propositions. But
'research programmes' in economics have such *very* long lives.
In fact, exactly what are these 'budding research programmes'
which were so 'naively' and unjustifiably threatened? It might
be said that 'orthodox' economics, in the two hundred years
since Adam Smith, has consisted largely of a single 'research
programme' of building and qualifying self-adjusting models.
In monetary and 'macro'-economics the rival 'research programmes' of the quantity theory of money and of the income,
'aggregate demand', or 'Keynesian' theories, could be said to
have been 'budding' for over two hundred years. The orthodox
'research programme', or theory, of the firm has surely been
'budding' since Cournot wrote nearly 140 years ago. The
general equilibrium 'research programme' has only been budding for just a century: or could Lakatos have been referring
to the comparatively recent 'research programmes' of growth-
modelling? Or that of the radical 'chiconomics' of the empirically vacuous Cambridge capital analysis and the Sraffa
models? It is impossible to say, since Lakatos gave no examples.
In fact it seems difficult to escape the suspicion that Lakatos's
'naively' and unfairly threatened, 'budding research programmes' in economics are as insubstantial, or even mythical,
as Sir Karl's 'Newtonian revolution'. Taking a critical look at
the history of political economy and economics one simply
fails to find timorous, cautious economists hastily retreating
and abandoning their 'budding research programmes' to the
first crude and 'cruel' attacks of 'naive' and undiscriminating
falsificationists. Quite the reverse, and dangerously and even
reprehensibly so. The history of the subject is, in fact, full of
exaggerated theoretical claims put forward in order to sell particular professed policies of one political stripe or another; and
these claims have often been tenaciously and dogmatically
maintained, with the aid of every kind of conventionalist
stratagem, for decades, and indeed half-centuries on end, re-

gardless of evidence or the lack of it. There may possibly be *some* justification for tenacity. But there is even more justification for sustaining criticism, on falsificationist principles, especially so long as these century-old (but still 'budding') programmes are being unjustifiably employed for the selling of questionable policies.

Perhaps Lakatos's remarks about 'budding research programmes' in economics should be interpreted in terms of his prescription that

> to give a stern 'refutable interpretation' to a fledgling version of a programme is dangerous methodological cruelty.[32]

Lakatos may have considered that the precepts of gentleness and patience, which he had argued for in the case of theoretical physics, were equally and automatically appropriate in the case of economic theory, in spite of the basic difference in the material, and consequently in the history and processes of 're-search programmes', in the two subjects. For Lakatos had developed his arguments against Popper's more severe, 'falsificationist' prescriptions as inappropriately destructive, *from the case of physics*, and had distilled his own more 'flexible' brand of 'falsificationism' from the history of physics. We are not attempting to criticise Lakatos's prescriptions on their home ground of theoretical physics. The question is how suitable and relevant these arguments are in the case of theoretical economics.

We should now consider the distinguished pioneer attempt by Dr. Latsis to apply the prescriptions of Lakatos to the criticism and appraisal of the theory of the firm. The critical approach of Dr. Latsis seemed to evolve somewhat as between his first article of 1972 and his Nauplion paper (1974). We would only call attention to what may be a detail in this evolution, but one which seems to be quite significant with regard to the applicability of the methodological prescriptions of Lakatos to economics. In his earlier article Dr. Latsis discussed Professor Machlup's defence of the orthodox theory of the firm and Machlup's criticism of destructive 'falsificationism'. Dr. Latsis described these criticisms by Professor Machlup as 'an almost complete anticipation of Lakatos's similar criticism'.[33]

In his later paper Dr. Latsis, after describing Machlup (and Friedman) as 'conventionalists', maintains that they wanted 'the neoclassical research programme' or orthodox theory of the firm.

> to come out as satisfactory when judged by *general* methodological standards; at least it should not be impatiently rejected at the behest of utopian norms.[34]

According to Dr. Latsis, Professor Machlup

> repeatedly argues that counter-intuitive and apparently refuted assumptions may nevertheless be valuable for explanation and prediction in neoclassical microeconomics.[35]

No attempt here is being made to deny all value to 'neoclassical microeconomics'. But Dr. Latsis then goes on to find, regarding Professor Machlup's criticism, that it is based on an 'interpretation of the neoclassical theory of the firm', which

> generates built-in defence mechanisms enabling the reconciliation of almost any recalcitrant evidence with the theory.

Moreover, Professor Machlup's interpretations of the assumptions of the 'theory'

> tell us nothing about the limits of applicability of the perfectly competitive model; they only tell us that the perfectly competitive model is only applicable when it can be applied.

Dr. Latsis goes on to maintain:

Since Machlup and other neoclassical economists are either

reluctant or unsuccessful in spelling out in advance the specific circumstances in which their models are applicable, any adverse evidence whatsoever can be attributed to 'special circumstances'.

Dr. Latsis concludes regarding 'conventionalism':

Conventionalist methodology is, as we have indicated, peculiarly suited to account for the appraisals of economists. Direct empirical confrontation of the theory's postulates with lower level statements is excluded, i.e. clashes between the theory's consequences and experiential statements, are accommodated by means of a battery of conventionalist stratagems. Finally, those empirical successes, if any, which the theory secures are hailed as triumphs and used as arguments for putting up with its intuitive implausibility and its empirical deficiencies.[36]

This is an admirably perceptive, precise, and penetrating criticism (and quite as 'destructive' as any bloodthirsty 'falsificationist' would want to be). It should only be added that in its treatment of 'conventionalism', and the stratagems thereof, it seems to be entirely and centrally Popperian. Also especially welcome is Dr. Latsis's conclusion regarding the key problem of sorting out 'the genuine (or justified) defense manoeuvres from the *ad hoc* ones':

Falsificationism may be very useful here. For instead of attempting to knock out theoretical systems by furnishing empirical counter-examples we may employ falsificationist criteria to rule out defensive manoeuvres that are unacceptable.[37]

One is simply left wondering about the almost completely Lakatosian nature of the *criticism* of falsificationism put forward by Professor Machlup, if Machlup's methodological criteria allowed or encouraged the extensive use of the conventionalist tactics so trenchantly criticised by Dr. Latsis.

One cannot show that the testability principle of Popper should be replaced in economics by the prescriptions of Lakatos, by proceeding to deal justly and destructively, by means of Popperian criteria, with the historical examples one selects. Not much significance can arise *for economics* in the revisions of Popper by Lakatos, if all, or virtually all, economic 'programmes' are either vulnerable – or approved – *both* according to Popper's principles, *and* according to those of Lakatos. To justify the replacement of Popper's prescriptions by those of Lakatos in economics one must set out in precise terms, from the history of economics, an example of a 'budding research programme' which went on subsequently to a fruitful or illuminating career, and which would have been allowed through uncriticised by the more discriminating Lakatos prescriptions, but which would have been unjustly and prematurely attacked by Popper's testability criterion. At the same time it should be shown that the more flexible prescriptions would not, in practice, in economics, be reduced to 'anything goes'. Such a demonstration does not seem yet to have been performed and would seem inherently rather difficult to perform.

We come now to an acutely interesting point suggested by Lakatos, although he only just touches upon it without specifically mentioning economics. This is his brief intimation that methodological prescriptions may need to be enforced more explicitly or less explicitly according to the degree of 'immaturity' or 'maturity' of the subject.

According to Lakatos:

While Polanyite academic autonomy should be defended for departments of theoretical physics, it must not be tolerated, say, in institutes of computerised social astrology, science planning or social imagistics.

In fact, Lakatos goes on to enquire:

Is it not then *hubris* to try to impose some *a priori* philosophy of science on the most advanced sciences?[38]

Lakatos seems to suggest here that while a kind of methodological autonomy should be tolerated for *some* subjects, or advanced sciences like theoretical physics, on which it would be '*hubris*' to seek to impose methodological precepts, there are other subjects whose claims to autonomy '*must not be tolerated*', and whose procedures it is by no means *hubris* to criticise from outside. Lakatos does not explicitly place economics in respect of this distinction of his. He mentions such intellectual phenomena as 'computerised social astrology' and 'social imagistics' as coming clearly on the wrong side of the tracks, as presumably would 'computerised *economic* astrology', which can certainly be said to exist.[39]

The question, therefore, arises as to how far the claims of such subjects to 'Polanyite autonomy' should be accepted. Perhaps Lakatos's Royal Society for the Prevention of Cruelty to Budding Research Programmes should prosecute any naively destructive critic of the procedures of such subjects? Should, it might be asked, critics of the 'Marxist' research programme, which, in various forms (such as the Stalinist 'research programme', much praised by some famous economists), has been now 'budding' for over a century (and the criticism of which was the original starting-point of Popper's falsificationist prescriptions), *also* be prosecuted for cruelty to 'budding research programmes'? Just when would a prosecution for 'cruelty' be in order and when not?

Indeed there may well be some economists who would be eager to claim, by a kind of Polanyite UDI, the 'mature', 'developed', or 'advanced' condition, which would entitle them, according to Lakatos, to what he called 'Polanyite autonomy' – like theoretical physicists – on whom it would be *hubris* to seek to impose the critical standards of 'some *a priori* philosophy of science', and whose budding research programmes it would be culpable cruelty to criticise on falsificationist lines.

Lakatos's own 'criteria of adequacy', or his methodological prescriptions, have been described from differing viewpoints as completely, or irrationally, lax by both Feyerabend and Kuhn. Professor Feyerabend has even maintained:

E

Scientific method, as softened up by Lakatos, is but an ornament which makes us forget that a position of 'anything goes' has in fact been adopted.[40]

It may be emphasised that (a) no view is being expressed here as to whether Professor Feyerabend's description of Lakatos's precepts is accurate or not; nor (b) is it being argued that, in any case, a methodological doctrine of 'anything goes' might not be tolerable or appropriate *for theoretical physics and similar subjects*, from the history and philosophy of which this prescription has been derived. What is asserted here is that *it would be far more difficult to prevent Lakatos's prescriptions being reduced to 'anything goes' or to something practically indistinguishable, in economics,* even though it might not be intended or admitted that such total permissiveness should result. It seems that the essential distinctions, or tools, of Lakatos, may be too finely calibrated for handling adequately the softer and more inchoate intellectual material of which economic 'research programmes' consist. The Lakatos prescriptions may not in economics, provide sufficiently clear-cut scientific choices or decisions. Moreover, testing in economics, as compared with physics, tends to be so much more ambiguous, uncertain, and inconclusive in its results, partly because the phenomena being tested are liable to historical change.

Lakatos himself expressed alarm at the permissive irrationalism' which he considered, rightly or wrongly, would be, and had been, encouraged by Kuhn's earlier views:

> If *even in science* there is no way of judging a theory but by assessing the number, faith and vocal energy of its supporters, then *this must be even more so in the social sciences*: truth lies in power. Thus Kuhn's position would vindicate, no doubt, unintentionally, the basic political *credo* of contemporary religious maniacs ('student revolutionaries')[41]

Needless to say, Kuhn flung the charge of encouraging

'irrationalism' back at Lakatos, and certainly a doctrine of 'anything goes' would open the gates for the exponents of 'truth is power'. It is not necessary here to try to assess whether it was Kuhn or Lakatos who was bringing the more unjustified charge against the other. But attention should be called to *Lakatos's explicit distinction between 'science' on the one hand, and 'the social sciences' on the other hand*. Lakatos seems to be arguing – with much validity – that different degrees of stringency in applying or enforcing methodological prescriptions may be necessary for *'the social sciences'* (including economics), as contrasted with 'science' proper. For a formula or strategy which might be adequate in theoretical physics, where today the danger from the exponents of 'truth lies in power' is hardly acute, might be disastrously inadequate in the social sciences, in which rule by 'number, faith and vocal energy' (or by sheer physical violence as on some 'university' campuses) is a prospect or possibility not lightly to be dismissed.

It is obvious that the difficulties of testing, or falsifying, are generally incomparably greater in economics than in physics. In the social sciences the ratio of conjectures to refutations – the plethora of conjectures and the paucity of refutations – is significantly higher. Theories and 'programmes' in economics and the social sciences tend to have extremely long lives, surviving often in a stagnant or semi-moribund condition. They hardly need any anxious protection against 'cruelty' or 'impatience', many of them resisting the worst their critics can do for decades, or even centuries, on end. In fact, in the social sciences and economics, intellectual over-population is a chronic condition. So also are wildly over-confident claims, pretensions, and applications, from the more exuberant 'classicals' to our 'growth' experts of a century and a half later; and so also may now be the threats of the violent propagandists of the idea that 'truth lies in power'. It must be weighed up how far the doctrine of 'truth lies in power' might not be fostered and facilitated by the vetoing of attempts to seek falsifiable formulations, even with regard to the most dubious among the excess population of unrefuted conjectures.[42]

VI

In conclusion we may turn briefly to Lakatos's suggestion about the reluctance of economists to accept Popper's methodological criteria and prescriptions. As noted earlier, one must distinguish between the vitally important issues of Popper's general methodological principles, and his highly over-optimistic, but more-or-less incidental, comments regarding a 'Newtonian revolution' in economic theory, and the comparability of economic laws with those of physics. Such comments as these latter are bound to be highly popular with 'theoretical' economists and their influence could probably be shown to have been quite important in the fifties and early sixties.[43] But as regards Sir Karl's general methodological principles, there is some justification for Lakatos's claim that economists have been reluctant to accept them. Of course at one time Popper's name was often invoked and a good deal of fair-weather lip service was paid to the principles of empirical testability and falsifiability. But when it was discovered that to press home such prescriptions or criteria might be disconcertingly destructive from the point of view of 'professional' status or particular cherished dogmas, Popper's name became rather unfashionable with economists and their methodological spokesmen.

For the kind of 'methodology' which many economists want and value is one that boosts up their prestige – vital for raising funds – as 'Scientists' with a capital 'S', while being flexibly permissive, barring no holds, or even letting 'anything go', when it comes to throwing one's weight around in the political arena as a professional 'expert' on behalf of one's particular favourite policies.[44] Alfred Marshall said that economists ought to be suspicious of, and critically inclined towards, all policies popular with politicians and the public.[45] Similarly, philosophers of science and methodological critics should be suspicious of methodological claims and prescriptions which are popular with economists.

However, although Lakatos's generalisation regarding economists' 'reluctance' to accept Popper's methodological prescriptions is not without justification, it should, on the other side, be recognised that they have exercised at least *some* significant impact on economics in recent decades. It is not *quite* so easy today, as it was before Popper's prescriptions began to gain ground, to dismiss entirely the principle of testability or refutability, in spite of the difficulties of its application in practice. It has been a major item on the credit side (countering a certain amount on the debit side) in the development of econometrics, that it has, up to a point, brought a wider recognition of the principle of testability. As Professor Samuelson has said:

> In connection with the exaggerated claims that used to be made in economics for the power of deduction and *a priori* reasoning – by classical writers, by Carl Menger, by the 1932 Lionel Robbins (first edition of *The Nature and Significance of Economic Science*), by disciples of Frank Knight, by Ludwig von Mises – I tremble for the reputation of my subject. Fortunately we have left that behind us.[46]

Though rather severe on one or two of those mentioned, this judgment is substantially justifiable. It must be, to a considerable extent, ascribed to the influence of Popper's prescriptions that we have left *some* of that behind. In fact, Popper's prescriptions and criteria, in spite of his main interests being focused on theoretical physics, had one of their origins or starting-points in the epistemological problems of 'social science', or, more specifically were devised to counter the claims to omniscience and irrefutability of a degenerate 'Marxism'.[47] From this original source of theirs, Popper's doctrines derive a certain relevance to the problems of the social sciences not shared by doctrines or prescriptions which have been entirely derived and distilled from the history and problems of theoretical physics.

But in spite of a tendency to some kinds of improvement, new and old forms of the kind of intellectual malpractices which Popper's prescriptions were designed to combat are still widespread in economics: 'verbalism', 'conventionalist' and 'immunising' stratagems, and the erosion of testable formulations and testing. It has long been taken for granted by many economists and complacent methodologists that no criticisms of the 'assumptions' underlying models, which would require their testing or testability, need to be heeded. As far as 'assumptions' are concerned, that virtually 'anything goes' is a pretty well-established practice: they may simply be 'plucked from the air', as Sir Henry Phelps Brown has put it. Similarly, among some economists, prediction, also, may now be rejected as a test of theories. Moreover the blurring of the empirical with the purely conceptual, or definitional, seems to continue almost unabated, at least until quite recently. It was not some pedantic methodologist, but the Economic Adviser to HMG, who complained:

> What I regard as a besetting sin among economists; that of enunciating purely definitional relationships when they purport to be making statements about reality.[48]

A variant of this kind of 'besetting sin' is prominent in the form of ambiguous, but obviously oversimplified, and insistently dogmatic propositions about what 'determines', or 'governs', saving and investment, or wages, etc. (a kind of ambiguous dogmatism cultivated by 'Keynesians'); or, on the other hand, oversimplified propositions about the 'cause' of inflation (favoured by 'monetarists').[49] Much of the steam in the Monetarist–Keynesian debate would fade away without this kind of dogmatic ambiguity, which could best be dealt with by a precise application of the falsifiability principle.

Certainly Popper's youthful difficulties with the constant confirmations of their theories discovered every day in the newspapers by 'Marxists', might be compared with Professor Patinkin's recent bewilderment over the almost unfailing stream of confirmations of their theories achieved by the leading rival schools of monetary theory:

What generates in me a great deal of skepticism about the state of our discipline is the high positive correlation between the policy views of a researcher (or, what is worse, of his thesis director), and his empirical findings. I will begin to believe in economics as a science when out of Yale there comes an empirical Ph.D. thesis demonstrating the supremacy of monetary policy in some historical episode – and out of Chicago, one demonstrating the supremacy of fiscal policy.[50]

We would emphasise, in conclusion, that no one has insisted or explained more clearly than Sir Karl that any methodological prescriptions for scientific decisions and investments must inevitably be based on certain ethical or political choices. The philosopher of science, no more than the economist, can lay down, for the kind of decision-makers or 'investors' with whom he is concerned, any general formula, with any significant degree of content and applicability, for absolutely and objectively 'rational' conduct in real-world conditions of uncertainty and ignorance. The attempt might be made to analyse the investment decisions, or the 'portfolio' of theories, the 'rational' scientist should take or hold, but no very practically informative formula would emerge. All that can be set out are 'reasonable' principles, or maxims, for scientific decision-making and investments which will not yield any uniquely correct answers and will inevitably need interpretation and judgment for their practical application. The principle of falsifiability is linked with what Popper calls 'fallibilism' as the epistemological basis for a free, pluralist society.[51] Watering down, disarming, or stifling this critical principle, by leaving the green light switched on permanently, signalling 'anything goes' for every kind of complacent, pretentious and noxious dogmatism would constitute a grand new *'trahison des clercs'*.[52]

Four

'Crisis' in the Seventies: the Crisis of Abstraction

1

With the approach of the second centenary of *The Wealth of Nations* much has been heard of some kind of 'crisis' in economics. Sir John Hicks has referred to one: so has Dr. Gunnar Myrdal: and so has Lady Robinson. However, the 'crisis' is apt to be located in one of *the other* brands, or schools, of the subject, not one's own. Agreement on the existence of a 'crisis' may be combined with complete disagreement as to its nature. It would certainly seem that there are various different factors contributing to the 'crisis' or critical situation.

The 'crisis', or 'crises', or – if one dislikes the term – the present position of or in, economics, has both its general, more or less world-wide, or cosmopolitan aspects, as well as its peculiarly and specifically local or British aspects. To some extent, but not entirely, corresponding with this distinction, one may separate the 'internal' and 'external' factors shaping the condition of (or 'crisis' in) economics: that is, those factors originating autonomously from *within* the subject and the development of its problems, and, on the other hand, those environmental factors arising from outside the intellectual problems of the subject itself, as do, to a large extent, the more specifically British aspects. Certainly the 'crisis', or critical situation in the subject seems especially, so far as Britain is concerned, to be somehow related to the persistent crisis in the economy and in economic policy. It seems to be assumed that because the problems of policy seem to be so intractable or insoluble, this, in itself, denotes a 'crisis' in *the subject*.[1] This conclusion does not completely follow. In so far as nothing approaching a coherent consensus may exist regarding the explanation of the changing behaviour of the economy, this may be said to constitute something of a crisis in the subject. But economics cannot, or should not, appropriately be described as undergoing a crisis simply because remedies or 'solutions' cannot be prescribed for current problems which would be generally acceptable to a public, or its political representatives, overfed on exaggerated expectations as to what government economic policies can deliver.

II

According to some theories of business cycles, a 'crisis' phase inevitably follows the preceding upswing or 'boom', and the stronger or more extravagant the boom has been, the more severe is the succeeding crisis likely to be. In fact the crisis, painful though it might be, could be seen as a progressive process of 'break-through', when reality breaks through the extravagant illusions of the boom.

The developments often described as 'the Keynesian Revolution', first applied, with apparently much success, to British economic policy in war-time, were followed or accompanied after the war by relatively *very* high and stable levels of employment. The appalling and overriding economic problem of Britain in the inter-war years seemed to have been removed. This sequence of events did much, in the decade or so after the war, to maintain a high and stable level of confidence among economists in Britain, and to promote the prestige of economics as a successful, progressive subject. Indeed, a certain distant parallel might, in some respects, be drawn between the nineteen-fifties and early sixties in Britain, and the roughly corresponding decades a century previously, when mid-Victorian prosperity, following upon the implementation of the main policy doctrines of the English Classical economists, promoted, until the late sixties and early seventies, such prestige for, and satisfaction with, in its country of origin, the Classical version of 'the Science of Political Economy'.[2] Both Classical political economy and Keynesian economics were, in fact, largely insular in origin and influence, even, to some extent, eccentrically so (though the former was probably rather more so than the latter).

However, by the middle nineteen-fifties the problem of Britain's low rate of growth had appeared and seemed to provide an opportunity to repeat the Keynesian triumph over unemployment. The 'growth' problem was very much discovered by economists, rather than being one of which ordinary people were directly conscious like unemployment and inflation. But 'growth' was eagerly seized upon by politicians. In fact 'growthmanship' emerged very much as the answer to politicians' prayers. All their schemes and promises to extract a pint and a half out of a pint pot could be rationalised and legitimised by invoking the upsurge of 'growth', which some economists were not slow to claim confidently they knew how to produce – even up to doubling previous British rates – by 'purposive' planning and direction.

III

In addition to these 'external' factors a further boost to confidence and prestige was generated by the quantitative, or mathematical, 'revolution'. This was *apparently* an 'internal' phenomenon, arising out of the development of the subject itself (though a sceptic might suggest that 'external' factors involving an eager quest for 'professional' status and prestige had a large part in this development). Anyhow, the quantitative and mathematical revolution was not a mainly or specifically British phenomenon. It was rather an import from the United

States, which was certainly made the most of by its exponents on the eastern side of the Atlantic and considerably impressed some schools of economists, as well as some philosophers of science, in Britain. Even the keenly critical Sir Karl Popper was so carried away as to discern a 'Newtonian revolution' in mathematical economics. According to some of the exponents of this revolution, economics could now, for the first time, be regarded as genuinely 'scientific', comparable epistemologically with the natural sciences (just as James Mill and Ricardo, nearly a century and a half before, had claimed for the 'laws' of their new science the same degree of certainty as was recognised for those of Newton and even Euclid). It was explained how, in the sixties, 'the character of the subject changed from being an art to an applied science'.[3]

The kind of pretensions entertained by the more eager public relations officers of this particular 'revolution', including its Youth-Movement aspects, was rather pithily expressed in a chapter on 'Economists and the Scientific Revolutionaries' in a widely-used micro-economics text:

> Science, of course, belongs naturally to the young. But particularly is this true of scientific revolutions. The field we are about to enter will serve as an example of the new science, and some of its brilliant young practitioners are beautiful examples of the scientific revolutionary. . . They are mathematicians of the new kind, preoccupied with issues of form. . . Some of what is revolutionary in science is being done by economists. This is clearly very new: under the old régime economists never made it as scientists. . . Of course, economists always *wanted* to be taken seriously as scientists. In the old days, however, things were hard for them. . . The very (admitted) weaknesses of economics as a science in the old days make its new strengths all the more glaring examples of what is new on the scientific scene in general.[4]

IV

Moreover, as an overwhelmingly positive and quantitative proof of the remarkable 'progress' in the subject in the late fifties and early sixties in Britain, a veritable explosion of economics took place not only in universities, to which for nearly a century it had been mainly confined, but in schools, colleges, industry, banking, and in all branches of government. In all these areas, whatever index-numbers were used, the growth-rate was truly phenomenal. This indeed was Britain's 'Economics Miracle'. If the rate of growth of the economy seemed unresponsive to 'expert' treatment, at least a truly impressive rate of growth in the number of economists and students of the subject could be registered.[5]

This remarkable quantitative upsurge in Britain was summarised, as follows, with apparently considerable pride and satisfaction, by the President (1974) of the Royal Economic Society. Between 1962 and 1974:

> The number of economists employed by universities has probably trebled; the number teaching the subject in schools has risen still faster; those employed by business have multiplied sixfold or more; the number of economists employed by the Government has increased – admittedly from a low base – some ten- to twenty-fold according to the definitions used.[6]

These developments were assumed, with remarkable confidence, by the President of the Royal Economic Society to demonstrate

> a very strong 'revealed preference' for our services... The demand curve for economists in real terms has shifted very sharply to the right.[7]

The vital and central upsurge was in the universities, until recently the sole or the main forum of the subject. Here the great increase took place in a period of hectic expansionist empire-building throughout most or all departments and faculties in the universities, in which the creation and maintenance of empires depended on pulling in the crowds.[8] Obviously there was a danger, which does not seem (judging by some textbooks of the period) in fact to have been avoided, of overselling the subject, both in terms of its rigorous 'scientific' characteristics and its immediate, practical 'fruit-bearing' potential. However, the emergence, for the first time in Britain, of large numbers of economists *practising* the subject, in the real world of business and government, rather than simply or mainly lecturing, teaching, writing and arguing about it in classrooms or academic specialist journals, was liable, in due course, to be followed by a kind of critical 'feedback', to the educational centre, regarding the relevance of the economic education which was being purveyed. It had long seemed somewhat incongruous, especially in Britain, that a subject apparently with such close, real-world practical intentions and applications should be cultivated almost entirely within the groves of academe, or by those only temporarily released therefrom, and that an 'economist' meant *almost* exclusively, *in Britain, at any rate*, down to about the early sixties, a don or an academic. Now this strange imbalance began to alter. On the side of government and business policies it could hardly be maintained that any hopes of a rapid, discernible improvement were fulfilled. But in the reverse direction, this development might well, by means of a realistic feedback, favour the long-term health of academic economics.[9]

V

Rather suddenly, amid the rush of these remarkable developments, there began to be audible in the early seventies sounds of dissension and disquiet, even loud proclamations of scepticism. A yawning credibility gap (at least as some leading authorities seemed to perceive it) opened up regarding the British Economics Miracle. Moreover, the protests emanated not from 'angry young men', or dissatisfied 'young Turks', eager to do down a complacent 'establishment', but from the most senior establishment figures such as the President of the Royal Economic Society (1972), the Director of the National Institute for Social and Economic Research, and even one or two Nobel Laureates.

We may distinguish three main themes in the protests: *first*, that contrary to the traditional aims and claims of the subject, which had not been admittedly or explicitly abandoned, much of the most highly-regarded work in economics was not making, and did not seem at all designed to make, any useful contribution to increasingly pressing real-world problems (although this was hardly ever explicitly admitted).

Secondly, there were protests directed at the prevalence, prestige and quantity of much work based on an extreme, undisciplined and unjustifiable degree of abstraction.

A *third* theme, which we may briefly discuss later, is that of the desirability of educational changes with more of a place for history in economics curricula.

It might be asked why these protests and complaints had not been heard before. For what was being complained of in the state of economics had been chronic for a long time in Britain. As regards the considerable extent that this had been the case, 'better late than never' is the appropriate comment. But, to a considerable extent, also, recent 'external' developments in the form of rapid, startling, and partly world-wide institutional changes (especially, for example, the great upsurge of wage-claims and inflation after about 1969) showed up, as more serious and defective, abstractions and oversimplifications, which had existed before, but which it had been possible to take less seriously. However, the British laments for the state of economics were undoubtedly *partly, and to a significant extent,* inspired by the state of the British economy and the failures of British economic policies, though similar complaints were to be heard from leading authorities in the United States.

VI

Anyhow, the authoritative complaints with which we are here concerned did not consist simply of general lamentations. We shall now quote some of the typical arguments. Though presumably these statements are quite widely known, it is very difficult to say, because of the absence of reactions to them, how far they really sank in or were taken seriously, or how far, on the other hand, their effect has been that of a shower of rain on ducks' backs.[10]

Regarding the traditional aims and claims of the subject, as the Director of the National Institute put it (with only slight and not unjustifiable exaggeration):

> All the great economists of the past have been reformers and *there are few contemporary economists who would not claim that their work and their ideas are intended to contribute in some degree, however indirectly, to the improvement of a firm, an industry, a national economy or the world as a whole.* And if it is said that some do not claim this, *there are very few who explicitly proclaim the uselessness of their work.*[11]

Set against this tradition the present extent and prestige of work based on extreme abstraction seems all the more striking. Of this work Sir Henry Phelps Brown, the President of the Royal Economic Society, complained:

> *I believe that it is impaired from the first by being built upon assumptions about human behaviour that are plucked from the air.* That it proceeds by abstraction and builds models or follows paths of reasoning to reveal the outcome of assumptions, is in itself nothing against it, for doing this is a necessary part of the endeavour to understand any process, in human affairs no less than in physical. But what does impair it, scientifically and practically, is that the human

propensities and reactions it purports to abstract are not in
fact abstracted, that is to say drawn out from observations,
but are simply assumed – assumed out of everyday knowledge, or introspection, or convention, or the faith that
however unaccountably some people may behave on some
occasions, in the long run and for social aggregates it is
rational, maximising behaviour that prevails. . . *It is not
scientifically respectable*. The purpose is no longer to observe
and account for a particular situation or sequence of events,
the elements of the problem have not been drawn from
observation in the field. . .[12]

This complaint was expressed by Mr. Worswick as follows:

There now exist whole branches of abstract economic theory
which have no links with concrete facts and are almost
indistinguishable from pure mathematics. Indeed, it might
be more correct to say that there have come into being new
branches of mathematics whose distinguishing feature is
that some of the axioms and some of the terminology show
traces of the ancestry of this particular branch of mathematics, which originated in the distant past in some real
economic question. . . There is, I have suggested, at present
an imbalance among the specialisms which go to make
economic science. It would be too neat to say that progress
in economics occurs fastest in those areas which are furthest
removed from reality, but there is sufficient in the charge to
cause discomfort. *Too much of what goes on in economic
and econometric theory is of little or no relevance to serious
economic science.*[13]

This same complaint received weighty endorsement from the
Nobel Laureates, Professors Frisch and Leontief. In his
Presidential Address to the American Economic Association
(1970) Professor Leontief referred to

an uneasy feeling about the present state of our discipline

[which] has been growing in some of us who have watched its unprecedented development over the last three decades. This concern seems to be shared even by those who are themselves contributing successfully to the present boom. They play the game with professional skill but have serious doubts about its rules.

However, according to Professor Leontief:

The feeling of dissatisfaction with the present state of our discipline which prompts me to speak out so bluntly seems, alas, to be shared by relatively few.

Professor Leontief's basic complaint was that of Sir Henry Phelps Brown and Mr. Worswick:

Continued preoccupation with imaginary, hypothetical, rather than with observable reality has gradually led to a distortion of the informal valuation scale used in our academic community to assess and to rank the scientific performance of its members. . .
    In no other field of empirical inquiry has so massive and sophisticated a statistical machinery been used with such indifferent results.[14]

At about the same time the doyen of Econometrics, and Nobel Laureate, Professor Ragnar Frisch, condemned the widespread practice of what he called 'playometrics', which he compared with the intensive study of the shape of keyholes in thirteenth-century Iceland:

We should not mobilise an army of people to produce queer assumptions so to speak on the conveyor band and deduce consequences from these assumptions. If we do, we are on the wrong track both socially and scientifically, and we are not living up to our responsibilities. Such exercises may be an entertaining intellectual game. I admit that they are highly

F

entertaining and I can understand the great number of
students to whom this kind of exercise appeals. But it might
be a dangerous game both socially and scientifically.[15]

It must be conceded that on the positive side of the account
econometricians had contributed to winning some recognition
for the principle of empirical testability and refutability. On
the other side, as Mr. Worswick complained, much of the
elaborate apparatus they had concerned themselves with seemed
to be more or less useless:

> They are not, it seems to me, engaged in forging tools to
> arrange and measure actual facts so much as making a
> marvellous array of pretend-tools which would perform
> wonders if ever a set of facts should turn up in the right
> form. Thus what was said above about the detached
> mathematical nature of much economic theory also goes for
> some econometric theory as well.[16]

These comments regarding econometrics in Britain were
underlined by a remark of Professor H. G. Johnson, then at
the London School of Economics:

> The best work in econometrics done in the UK ... has been
> on the theory of econometrics *and not on what econometrics
> is supposed to be about*, namely, superior analysis and
> solution of important economic problems based on a
> combination of economics, mathematics and statistics.[17]

It must be emphasised that these complaints were by no
means directed simply, or even mainly, at 'neo-classical'
economics or 'micro'-economics, but even more seriously and
severely to growth modelling of all types and stripes (including,
especially, 'neo-Keynesian'). As Mr. Worswick argued:

> Anyone who has attempted to keep pace with even some
> small part of the enormous output of theoretical literature

must have asked himself at times, what exactly it is *about*? Consider as a first example the theory of economic growth, which has taken the form of the elaboration of a great variety of economic models whose behaviour is examined and whose performance is contrasted with that of other models. There is no question but that these models throw up fascinating problems, taxing one's intellectual powers to the full, but there is very little of it which is of any help in answering such questions as why growth rates differ among countries and between periods. Given the assumptions common to the models (no government, no international trade and so on), this is not surprising, and it may reasonably be argued that most model-builders have not been trying to do this anyway. But if not, what have they been trying to do? Facts hardly ever occur in this literature: the nearest we get is what Professor Kaldor has called stylised facts, which sometimes means no more than convenient assumptions without which determinate solutions of theoretical problems could not be obtained.[18]

On the subject of 'growth' models, Professor Ragnar Frisch also weighs in:

What is the economic relevance of intrinsic paths and the turnpike type of theorem of the kind I have mentioned? To be quite frank I feel that *the relevance of this type of theorem for active and realistic work on economic develop- ment, in industrialised or underdeveloped countries, is practically nil.* The reason for this is that the consequences that are drawn in this type of theorem *depend so essentially on the nature of the assumptions made.* And these assump- tions are frequently made for the convenience of mathe- matical manipulation than for reasons of similarity to concrete reality.[19]

VII

Lord Kaldor also contributed to these authoritative laments
with an article (1972) entitled 'The Irrelevance of Equilibrium
Economics'. It is of some interest, before we quote from this
article, to note the much less mature and critical view which
Lord Kaldor had taken of 'equilibrium economics' nearly forty
years earlier.[20] For these earlier, less mature arguments were
still to be found again, in the seventies, being deployed by
others in the defence of general equilibrium 'theory' against
Lord Kaldor.

In an early article (1934) on the theory of equilibrium Lord
Kaldor wrote:

A more rigorous formulation of the conditions under which
it is possible to make generalisations about the factors
determining economic equilibrium may be regarded as
*one of the main achievements of theoretical development
during the last fifty years* [i.e. 1884–1934]...

This development, according to Lord Kaldor, had led to

a purification of theory; to a more and more precise statement
of the conditions under which its generalisations can be
applied.[21]

Happily it had apparently not been necessary to pay *any*
price, in terms of relevance, for this much heightened 'rigour'
and 'purification':

*No one who studies it seriously would maintain that in
advancing along this path economics has gradually lost its
'relevance to facts'; or that economists, in their anxiety to
preserve the validity of their 'laws', have come increasingly
to neglect the operation of those forces which 'really matter'.
For in any analytical study, forces whose laws of operation*

are known must clearly be separated from others in whose behaviour no such 'uniform principles' have yet been detected; and the only satisfactory way to detect and account for the influence of the latter in the real world is by assuming them away and examining what events would be like in their absence... *All this is clearly in accord with the main canons of scientific analysis; it is the only procedure to adopt...*[22]

In spite of it being 'the only procedure to adopt': in spite of its accord 'with the main canons of scientific analysis': in spite of the increased 'rigour' (a claim still much in vogue): in spite of the 'laws', the 'uniform principles', and the rest, somehow over the years this programme, according to Lord Kaldor's own riper judgment, has not worked out: the method or programme seems to have been wrong from the start. After nearly forty years of a kind of intellectual maturation-process, Lord Kaldor (1972) proclaimed:

> The powerful attraction of habits of thought engendered by 'equilibrium economics' has become a major obstacle to the development of economics as a *science*...
> The latest theoretical models, which attempt to construct an equilibrium path through time with all prices for all periods fully determined at the start under the assumption that everyone foresees future prices correctly to eternity, require far more fundamental 'relaxations' for their applicability than was thought in the original Walrasian scheme. The process of removing the 'scaffolding' as the saying goes – in other words of *relaxing* the unreal basic assumptions – has not yet started. Indeed, the scaffolding gets thicker and more impenetrable with every successive re-formulation of the theory, with growing uncertainty as to whether there is a solid building underneath.[23]

In a further criticism of abstraction in 'neo-classical' economics Lord Kaldor argued:

It is the hallmark of the neo-classical economist to believe that, however severe the abstractions from which he is forced to start, he will 'win through' by the end of the day – bit by bit, if he only carries the analysis far enough, the scaffolding can be removed, leaving the basic structure intact. In fact, these props are *never* removed; the removal of any one of a number of them – as for example, allowing for increasing returns or learning by doing – is sufficient to cause the whole structure to collapse like a pack of cards.[24]

This criticism seems to some extent justified. The point which, however, must be added is that it applies not only, nor most seriously, to 'neo-classical' equilibrium analysis, but *far more comprehensively and far more damagingly to the recent analysis by Lord Kaldor's colleagues, Dr. P. Sraffa and Lady Robinson.*[25] In fact the procedure which Lord Kaldor describes and condemns was long ago explicitly championed as what she called 'the optimistic method' by Lady Robinson in one of her first publications (1932), and deployed again in her *Introduction to Modern Economics* (1973).

By 'optimism' Lady Robinson meant a readiness to start from highly or extremely simplified and abstract assumptions in the hope that eventually one would somehow 'win through by the end of the day' (as Lord Kaldor puts it) by gradually inserting some of the more realistic complications, so that eventually some valid structure, serviceable in explaining real-world problems, will be found to stand up on its own, without the initial oversimplificatory 'scaffolding'. As Mrs. Robinson (1932) described it:

> Often one set of assumptions will be manageable, and the other realistic. The choice between them is then one of temperament, not one of opinion. Generally speaking, the optimistic, analytical English, economist will choose the manageable set.[26]

The choice of assumptions being a matter of 'temperament',

Mrs. Robinson maintained that 'there is no need to argue about it'.

To the objection that his (or her) assumptions are oversimplified the 'optimistic' economist must answer:

> I know very well that the world to which my technique applies is not the real world, but I am one of the optimistic economists, and when I have got well used to using my two-dimensional technique I will try to evolve a three-dimensional or an n-dimensional technique. . .
>
> The optimistic economists must get all the results which are just as complicated, but no more complicated, than their technique can produce hoping gradually to build up a more and more complicated technique as time goes by.[27]

Time has certainly 'gone by' since 1932. However (except that Lord Kaldor and others are beginning to express some rather unfair impatience) in the words of the old song: 'It's still the same old story'. The old 'neo-classical' cards have long ago been thrown away by Lady Robinson. But in spite of proclaiming that 'it is time to go back to the beginning and start again', in her textbook of 1973 she was still inviting her beginner-pupils to the same old 'optimistic' game of Spot the Relevance ('now you see it, now you don't'). This time there was apparently to be a new deal with a new pink pack of cards (though closer inspection revealed that the new pink pack contained many of the more important cards in the old 'neo-classical' pack). Still following closely in 1973 her 'optimistic' programme of 1932, and promising, apparently, that, as time went by, at the end of the day, they will win through, Lady Robinson (and Mr. Eatwell) explain to their students:

> to set up the simplest possible model and make use of it to illustrate all the relations that it is capable of showing, pointing out the problems that have been excluded as we go along. When we have got all we can out of the simplest model, we introduce another more complicated one and so build the argument from stage to stage.[28]

But just why, it is well worth asking, has the 'optimistic' method failed, on the whole, to 'win through by the end of the day', or just why does it seem impossible ever to take away the 'scaffolding' which, on the contrary (according to Lord Kaldor), seems to get denser and more impenetrable? It is certainly possible to spotlight precisely one piece of 'scaffolding', or one oversimplification, which has always been especially crucial and central to a very large part of basic, economic analysis and model-building, which it is *extremely* difficult, and has, in fact, proved impossible, to replace by a *general* model which is less oversimplified and which takes account of real-world problems, rather than assuming them out of existence. This is a more fundamental assumption than that which excludes increasing returns. Let us take Mrs. Robinson's account of 1932:

> The fundamental assumption on which the present simple technique of analysis is that each individual person acts in a sensible manner from the point of view of his own economic interests. The striking unreality of this assumption has sometimes tempted economists to deny that they are making it. . .[29]

Mrs. Robinson went on to agree that if this assumption was not valid and individuals acted 'in an unpredictable manner', or 'from a wide range of complicated motives', then this simple assumption and 'technique of analysis' would prove inadequate. However:

> Meanwhile the optimistic economists are working out their analysis on the simple assumption, and resolutely refusing to despair of evolving in the future a technique which will allow them to assume the existence of whatever other human motives have an influence in the economic sphere.[30]

Mrs. Robinson did not get right the main point about the 'fundamental assumption', which is not so importantly one of motive, but of *knowledge*. 'Acting in a sensible manner from the point of view of one's economic interests' was a quite inadequate way of stating 'the fundamental assumption', which must involve not only acting in such a way but *with full knowledge or correct expectations. This postulate has probably been the most important and pervasive single simplification, bearing more logical weight than any other, in the whole range of economic theorising, analysis, or model-building.* It is crucially involved with assumptions about equilibrium, or a tendency thereto, and with the fundamentals of monetary theory. It is certainly an extreme oversimplication or 'strong case', to use the phrase of Ricardo, the great founder of the 'optimistic' method.

The limitations imposed by this fundamental simplification, excluding ignorance and uncertainty, seem first to have been emphasised by Cliffe Leslie in his remarkable essay 'The Known and the Unknown in the Economic World' (1879).[31] Carl Menger briefly observed in his *'Investigations'* (1883) the serious limitations involved in assuming away error and suggested that historical critics should have pressed the point further. By far the fullest and most explicit exposure of the assumption of certainty was made by Frank Knight in his *Risk, Uncertainty and Profit* (1921). Keynes in his very first published article on economics (1910) had emphasised the importance of ignorance and uncertainty for any adequate theory of investment[32] and returned to the point, with great emphasis, in *The General Theory*. In the thirties several writers drew attention to this fundamental oversimplification.[33] But it has been quite remarkable how much of economic 'theorising' has proceeded blithely on regardless of the extreme limitations of assuming out of existence most of the problems of real-world decision-making. Only quite recently has this fundamental oversimplification come under more critical scrutiny, often for the purpose of attacking 'neo-classicism', it being conveniently overlooked how far the 'radical' critics themselves use the same, or a similar, assumption, for the purposes of such concepts as 'normal profit'.

Anyhow, the maximisation-under-certainty postulate has proved, as a piece of simplificatory scaffolding, *very* difficult, or virtually impossible, to remove, while leaving standing any model or theory for which any significant degree of generality could be claimed. There is simply no *general* assumption to replace this oversimplified one. For there is, so to speak, only one set of correct expectations, or state of adequate knowledge, for each and every situation. But there is an endless variety of incorrect and inadequate ones, which are constantly changing, and impossible to generalise about except in arbitrary terms. One may well start by focusing on the simplified 'strong' case and work out the implications of maximisation under certainty. But if one wishes to get any further and allow for the complicating features on which many real-world problems depend, then one has to introduce *some* ignorance and uncertainty, or *some* kind of expectations which are not fully correct. The question is *what particular kind*, from the virtually infinite possible range and variety? Correct expectations, and adequate knowledge, can only be correct and adequate. Incorrect expectations can be over-optimistic, over-pessimistic, too static, too elastic or too volatile, in an endless variety of different ways. Like Tolstoy's unhappy families, incorrect expectations are all unhappy (or incorrect) in their own different ways, while all correct expectations resemble one another in being in accord with their own particular conditions.[34] *It is bound to be more or less arbitrary, and involve 'plucking one's assumptions from the air' (as Sir Henry Phelps Brown puts it), to assume any one particular form of incorrect expectations or ignorance, as a general case. In fact it will be invalid to claim significant generality for an assumption of a particular form of ignorance, which can only be useful in dealing not with a general, but a particular historical case, which has been studied in detail empirically.* Of course, a virtually infinite number of 'models' can be constructed, based on assumptions of every conceivable kind of expectations and knowledge (or rather ignorance). But unless set up for explaining simply particular historical episodes, and based on appropriate empirical evidence, such 'models', or the basic assumption on which they are built, are likely to be highly arbitrary. That is why the maximisation-under-certainty assumption, claiming a kind of generality, even if of a vastly oversimplified kind, has so long retained its crucial role as 'scaffolding' and is likely to remain as such. But with regard to 'relaxing' this particular oversimplification according to the 'optimistic' programme, the procedure simply has not worked and does not seem likely to work. Not that it was not worth while to elaborate quite fully and precisely the oversimplified case of maximising under certainty.[35] But to continue decade after decade, or even half-century after half-century, with endless elaborations and refinements of this particular oversimplification hardly seems any longer a promising or progressive programme. Nor does the endless elaboration and refinement of particular more or less arbitrarily chosen alternatives from the virtually infinite range of possibilities, without empirical evidence of their real-world importance.

VIII

The laments for economics of the Nobel Laureates, the President of the Royal Economic Society, the Director of the National Institute and others, seemed to receive very little in the way of an answer. Unfortunately this cannot be taken to imply that the criticisms sank in, or were likely to have taken effect at all widely or deeply. One defence, however, which concentrated on general equilibrium 'theory', was forthcoming from Professor F. H. Hahn in an article with the title 'The Winter of Our Discontent' (1973).[36]

This defence may have seemed to come somewhat strangely from Professor Hahn, since only three years previously he had been taking a line not dissimilar from Lord Kaldor's later, more mature and critical views regarding equilibrium 'theory'. Professor Hahn (1970) had then seemed to regard the reasons for the actual considerable concentration on equilibrium 'theory' as *highly* dubious:

Of course, one of the reasons why *so much of our effort* is devoted to the study of equilibria is that they are singularly well suited to study. We all know the *endless variety* of adjustment models, not uncongenial to commonsense, one is capable of constructing.

However, after claiming that recent achievements of economic theory were 'in many ways beautiful', Professor Hahn allowed:

It cannot be denied that there is something *scandalous* in the spectacle of *so many people* refining the analyses of *economic states which they give no reason to suppose will ever, or have ever come about. It is probably also dangerous.*

The danger, Professor Hahn pointed out, was of that most insidious, and recently highly damaging kind, which encourages people to harbour illusions about the extent of their knowledge and understanding:

The recent, fairly elaborate analysis of the optimal plans for an economy which is always in equilibrium has, one suspects, *misled people to believe that we actually know how an economy is controlled.*[37]

(Incidentally, 'one suspects' also that, in the sixties, the fashionable proliferation of analytical growth 'models' and growth 'paths' may have 'misled people to believe' that they actually knew how to promote the growth of the British economy.)

Professor Hahn concluded:

It certainly is hard to find a justification for *the great preoccupation of both research and teching with equilibrium economics* unless one is also prepared to believe in, at least, a Marshallian tendency to equilibrium.

This is a very serious and penetrating line of criticism, which calls in question not necessarily the *total* utility of GE 'theory', from the start, with Walras, but, much more damagingly, the *marginal* utility of the continual elaborations and refinements of GE analysis in recent decades.

However, some three years later, contemplating what he described as his 'Winter of Discontent', Professor Hahn was to be found ardently and comprehensively *defending* general equilibrium 'theory' along similar lines to those which had been less maturely pursued by Lord Kaldor nearly forty years previously.

Professor Hahn began with one of those psychological, self-sealing defences to the effect that the critics of abstraction, or of general equilibrium 'theory' were from the start disqualified by their failure to understand what it was all about: 'they cannot understand what the best minds in their subject are saying'.[38]

Moreover, Professor Hahn made it clear that general equilibrium 'theory' was an extremely esoteric subject, apparently widely misunderstood and misinterpreted:

The vulgarizations of G E *which are the substance of most text-books of economics* are both scientifically and politically harmful.[39]

Furthermore, Professor Hahn took an early opportunity of warning his fellow-economists against the dangers of methodological criticism, or what he described as 'meddling with philosophy', or indulging in

epistemological speculation at which economists have shown themselves to be conspicuously bad.[40]

If this veto of Professor Hahn was to be taken seriously, it would, of course, effectively ward off almost *any* profound or penetrating criticism of GE 'theory' or anything else. One simply *has* to indulge in a certain amount of 'meddling with philosophy' (however 'conspicuously bad' one may be at it) unless one is to remain completely uncritical and complacent.

Naturally Professor Hahn himself then proceeds to 'meddle' repeatedly with philosophy (and much more dangerously for being, apparently, unaware that he is 'meddling').

The one piece of philosophical or epistemological 'meddling' which we must really insist on indulging in is to enquire urgently as to what sort of propositions GE theory produces (for example, regarding multiple equilibria etc., etc.)? Are these propositions to be regarded as purely definitional, not refutable empirically, or purely *logical* and analytical, to be appraised in terms of consistency (as they seem to be)? Or are they, in principle, *empirically* testable and refutable, possessing predictive content, to be appraised in terms of empirical evidence and empirical tests? Or are they some other type of proposition, and, if so, *just how are they to be examined and appraised*, or just what is the source of their validity (if they possess any)? Professor Hahn's defence of GE 'theory' seems largely to depend on confusion as to the answers to such questions, or regarding the nature of the propositions we are being asked to accept. For it is intellectually intolerable that these GE propositions should be claimed (1) to possess 'very great practical importance'; (2) to be correctly understood only by a few initiated specialists, since textbook interpretations are 'scientifically and politically harmful'; while (3) to probe into the epistemology of these GE propositions, or to insist on clarifying their nature, or how they may be appraised, is 'meddling with philosophy'. It seems that GE propositions must simply be taken or left, like 'beautiful' incantations. Such an attitude seems only too typical.

But Professor Hahn does not seek to defend GE 'theory' on the grounds that it is pure analysis, as pure mathematics might be defended; or on the grounds of its many 'beautiful' characteristics which he claimed to have discerned. *There may or might be a viable or valid line of defence for the activities of* GE *'theorists' along some such lines. But neither Professor Hahn nor anyone else has ever explicitly tried, in recent years, to formulate any such defence.* As Mr. Worswick said of economists (already quoted): 'There are very few who explicitly proclaim the uselessness of their work.'

On the contrary, Professor Hahn argues that GE 'theory' *'can be of very great practical importance'*, and *'of great practical significance'*.

He claims that GE 'theory' can make some kind of vital contribution to such issues, of certainly very great practical importance, as (a) flexible exchange rates; (b) exhaustible resources; and (c) the desirability or necessity of foreign aid.[41] But all that Professor Hahn succeeds in getting GE 'theory' to contribute is either the rather dubious countering of extraordinarily crude arguments for one side or the other, or the emphasising of logically conceivable (i.e. non-contradictory) possibilities without the suggestion of *any* empirical evidence that these possess the faintest real-world interest or significance.

In his earlier (1970) criticism of GE 'theory' Professor Hahn had very rightly insisted that the only valid reason for any special preoccupation with the logically conceivable position of equilibrium, must be a 'belief' that a tendency to this position existed in the real world. For this belief a certain amount of empirical evidence might reasonably be considered desirable. *But so it is with regard to any particular logically conceivable workings, or conditions, of exchange-rates*, for example, about which Professor Hahn describes the great contribution of GE 'theory' as being that the student thereof

> would note at once not only that there may be no equilibrium level, but also that if there is one such level there may be very many.[42]

Presumably these statements are not empirically testable or refutable. They simply announce one or two cases from an endless range of conceivable logical possibilities. If these particular cases have any real-world importance, or claim on the presumably scarce time of economists, there must be *empirical evidence*, or an *empirical* hunch, that they are *not merely* conceivable logical possibilities, but to some extent real-world actualities or probabilities of some significant degree. It is no contribution to economic policy-making *simply* to keep bringing

up what are merely particular conceivable logical possibilities from the quite endless range which logically exist, without
any evidence that there is some at least remote probability that
they actually occur.

This confusion of what may be logically, conceivably
'possible', with what is empirically significant or important, is
indeed a besetting sin among 'model' builders. They delight in
focusing and concentrating great attention on some logically
conceivable possibility (e.g. 'reswitching', multiple equilibria
etc.) without presenting any empirical evidence (or even seem-
ing to realise that such evidence might be desirable) that the
particular case they have fastened on has any claims on the
scarce time of someone concerned with the actual world, rather
than simply with the logic of conceptual manipulation.[43] The
onus must be very much on those who claim that the purely
taxonomic proclamation of a conceivable logical possibility is
of very great practical significance, to produce some empirical
evidence for their belief – as Professor Hahn, three years
previously, very rightly insisted was essential regarding the
equilibrium position.

Next we come to the great contribution which Professor
Hahn claims that GE 'theory' can make to refuting the proposition that

> we need not worry about exhaustible resources because they
> will always have prices which ensure their proper use.[44]

It surely cannot, in any case, amount to an important contribution to refute such a crude (though not self-contradictory)
formulation of the argument against government intervention
(if GE 'theory' does, indeed, refute it). Anyhow, the refutation
seems to consist of the remarkable *aperçu* that we are not all
omniscient about the future, a proposition which no economist
for the last half-century or more – if ever – ought to have needed
the assistance of GE 'theory' in order to grasp. The case for
relying (mainly or even entirely) on the price system *can* be
reasonably and coherently formulated (whether one agrees

with it, or not) in terms of the superior foresight of profit-motivated private individuals. But so formulated *it would itself possess empirical content and would require empirical evidence or argument to counter or refute it – not simply* GE *'theory' or, rather, hyper-abstract* GE *analysis.*

Similarly with regard to the case against foreign aid by governments as unnecessary, *'because* only investment profitable to private investors can be beneficial'.[45]

What *serious* economist, in the last hundred years, or, at any rate, since Pigou, has ever stated the argument in such extraordinarily crude terms and why should it be regarded as a supreme intellectual achievement, only possible for those equipped with the latest refined, rigorous analysis, to refute it? The practical contribution to the argument over the pros and cons of foreign aid which GE 'theory' can make, is in fact almost negligible. Quite serious arguments can be, and have been, developed against foreign aid (whether or not they are acceptable) and quite serious arguments can be developed *against* those arguments. But one can only enquire as to *the source, or basis, of criteria of 'practical importance'*, if GE theory's contribution to this debate is claimed to possess 'very great practical importance'.

IX

The two most significant implications of Professor Hahn's attempt at a defence of the abstractions of GE 'theory' are (1) that 'great practical importance', of a direct and immediate kind, for policy decisions, is claimed and set up as a basic criterion for the defence, while any arguments in terms of 'pure' science are spurned; and (2) there is much confusion and obscurity about what the implications for real-world practice and policy are, which can be derived from the extreme abstractions indulged in.

We would suggest that *we are confronted here with one of the most critical points, indeed the most critical, mainly*

G

*'internal' point, in the present 'crisis', or critical situation, in
economics. In fact, the 'crisis' in its internal aspects, might
well be described as a Crisis of Abstraction.* It is a 'crisis' of the
method of which Ricardo, tutored by James Mill, was the great
pioneer and exemplar, the introduction of which was his most
influential and far-reaching contribution: and this 'crisis'
centres especially around the knowledge postulate, which
Ricardo was probably the first explicitly to introduce.[46] Though
this crisis of abstraction may be regarded as *primarily* an internal phenomenon, it has also some external aspects or origins as
well. For the second, and *external* factor in the crisis of abstraction is the recent sharply increasing seriousness of social-
economic instability and interdependence, which have helped
to invalidate, increasingly profoundly, some of the long-stand-
ing abstractions on which the development of political economy
and economics have rested for much of their modern development (especially in Britain, which has, significantly, never so
far seen an influential development of historical or institutional
economics, as have most other leading countries). It may be,
and certainly *appears* to be, that certain social complications, or
interdependencies between 'social' and 'economic' institutions
and behaviour, have become much more significant, from
which it is much more arbitrary and unjustifiable to abstract, if
one is concerned with results applicable to real-world problems.

The *internal* factors which have brought on the crisis of
abstraction might be described as a kind of exhaustion of investment opportunity in intellectual terms. It may have once been
remunerative to work out the implications of, for instance, the
most important and pervasive of analytical abstractions, that of
maximisation under certainty. But when vastly increased numbers of economists go on, decade after decade, and half-century
after half-century, endlessly refining and elaborating on this
basic abstraction, or oversimplification, returns decline to nil –
not, of course, in terms of elaboration or refinement for its own
sake (in which there may well be no diminishing returns) but
in terms of anything useful for the explanation of real-world
problems or predictions. One cannot easily justify the extensive

cultivation of abstractions which have no discernible applicability or relevance to the world as it is, on the grounds that one day, somewhere or other, some kind of applicability or relevance might conceivably turn up.

Moreover, certain facile superficialities have become widely accepted as a defence of this preoccupation with oversimplified abstractions. *First*, from the platitude that *some* degree of abstraction is essential and inevitable in virtually any kind of scientific study, it seems to be presumed that *no* degree or kind of abstraction needs any defence or explanation: as regards abstract assumptions, anything goes: it's simply a matter of 'temperament', and there is no epistemological price to be paid. *Secondly*, there is the facile and frequent claim that it doesn't matter about the assumptions – however unrealistic they are – because the test comes with the predictions. But then one finds that the predictions, in their turn, are not very precisely or critically tested (if at all), and that there is a great deal of complacency regarding their adequacy for the guidance of decisions and policies.[47]

Of course, rules about abstraction, like any methodological rules, are relative to the aims and claims made for what emerges as 'results'. There is nothing illegal in endlessly elaborating and refining abstract 'models'. It is simply desirable to be clear about their interpretation in terms of real-world explanations and policy-contributions. And the question remains as to how far the results of these abstractions measure up to the traditional aims and claims of political economy and economics, which are very seldom openly repudiated, but, often implicitly or even explicitly, maintained.

In fact, a good deal of obscurity and ambiguity is to be met with on just these points regarding the empirical content, on the one hand, and the precise aims and claims, on the other, of all this apparently high-powered intellectual activity by those described as 'the best minds in the subject'. It is not simply, or necessarily, that these abstractions are entirely and inevitably useless – though they very often seem to be. It may well be that in some cases, if interpreted sufficiently discriminatingly and with extreme subtlety, they *might* be of *some* slight practical use in *some* cases. But they are usually very difficult to interpret and will often be misinterpreted.[48] In particular, so much concentration on abstract maxima and optima (or equilibria) has a damaging effect on policy discussion. This is not only for the cogent reason advanced by Professor Hahn (1970). The false suggestion is encouraged that such maxima or optima might, or ought, in some system or other, to be attainable. Such a suggestion fosters a deluded Utopianism and encourages quite unjust and misleading criticisms, from one side or the other, of rival economic systems.[49]

Let us now, however, emphasise that academics are certainly under no obligation to justify their work – any or all of it – according to a directly practical or policy-oriented criterion. Any suggestion that they should, which is heard with increasing frequency with the increasing centralisation of research funds under the government, must be vigorously resisted. Academics must always retain the right to pursue studies which are not of any immediate or discernible practical significance – a right which is essential and fundamental for academic freedom. This is not necessarily to allow that much abstract economic analysis can easily and obviously be defended by this, in principle, justifiable line of argument. Because one would be prepared to defend the study of Greek pottery of the fifth or sixth century BC, that does not mean, to cite Professor Frisch's example, that the study of Icelandic keyholes of the thirteenth, or any other, century, is defensible. Anyhow, no clear-cut boundary lines can be drawn here. But what is quite unjustifiable is *not* simply or necessarily that the teaching and research of a university person may have no, or only the most remote, practical significance, but that, implicitly or explicitly, *much* more practical significance is claimed for some kinds of work than they actually possess, or *much* richer fruits of practical significance are claimed or suggested than are in fact yielded.

However, the first great protest against excessive abstraction in political economy seems to have been that of Malthus against

Ricardo. Malthus claimed that 'the first business of philosophy is to account for things as they are'.

He went on:

> To know what can be done, and how to do it, is beyond a
> doubt, the most valuable species of information. The next to
> it is, to know what cannot be done, and why we cannot do it.
> The first enables us to attain a positive good, to increase our
> powers, and augment our happiness: the second saves us
> from the evil of fruitless attempts, and the loss and misery
> occasioned by perpetual failure.[50]

But Malthus might have added a *third* vital area of know-ledge, that is, with regard to *the limits of one's knowledge and the extent of one's ignorance* as to what can or cannot be done.

Extending or clarifying this third kind of knowledge may not appear as impressive a contribution as adding to knowledge of what can or cannot be done. But an increased and clearer knowledge of the extent of our ignorance can be vital and valuable in forestalling disappointment. Moreover, failure to increase, to the fullest possible extent, this kind of knowledge seems much less excusable than failure to extend the other more positive kinds. At the present juncture, a clearer under-standing of what can, and what cannot, be obtained by abstrac-tion is essential for obtaining a clearer and more accurate view of the limits of economic knowledge and the extent of economic ignorance – especially with regard to the baffling problems of economic policy. For as has been very cogently asked: 'Should not science be the more sceptical, the more desperately we want it to give us something nice?'[51] Furthermore, what Adam Smith himself said of medicine (or 'physic') two hundred years ago, may perhaps have some relevance for economists today:

> The presumption which commonly attends science must
> render it, in the practice of physic, ten times more dangerous

than the grossest ignorance when accompanied as it sometimes is, with some degree of modesty and diffidence.[52]

X

The 'crisis', or the problems, of abstraction in economics clearly
have important implications for the teaching of the subject.
There seems to have been a danger of economics being oversold,
in order to encourage beginners or pull in the crowds, by play-
ing down the quite heavy price in relevance which has to be
paid for the degree of abstraction which is being adopted.
Anyhow, the student is involved in a high degree of abstraction
from the very beginning of economic analysis. As soon as he
confronts the curves sweeping elegantly and impressively across
the blackboard or the pages of a textbook, he is liable to be
involved with the assumption of an extent and precision of
knowledge, or a freedom from ignorance and uncertainty,
which is, in fact, never possessed either by the real decision-
makers in a market, or by the economist. It may take a great
deal of persistent and quite delicate effort to get over to the
student the precise extent and nature of the limitations imposed
by such abstractions for real-world, or policy relevance. To use
a favourite term of Keynes, it may sometimes be easier to
'bamboozle' the student with abstractions, or at any rate, to
get him to accept, or make the willing suspension of disbelief,
than it is subsequently to 'debamboozle' him or her by bringing
home the full extent of the limitations for real-world relevance
and policy which the nature and degree of the abstractions
employed have inevitably imposed.

Moreover, there is a certain amount of economic analysis
taught at the third-year specialist undergraduate level, or to
graduates, which can hardly claim any relevance for explaining
or predicting real-world phenomena; or which, at any rate,
will never be of the slightest use, and may even be actively
misleading, for those trying to use economics in government or
business.

It used to be said, very unfairly, by rather philistine critics of a 'classical' education, that the only purpose or point served by teaching so much Latin and Greek was in order to have people qualified to teach Latin and Greek, in their turn, to others. It could be said, probably with rather less injustice of a certain amount of the more specialist teaching of economic analysis, that the only reason for teaching or learning so much of it must be for equipping people who can teach it to others. For this abstract analysis has no real-world use, though it is an accepted and even highly acclaimed part of specialist academic teaching. But evidence fed back from real-world users seems to be tending to suggest that the analysis which is actually useful, for a government adviser, for example, is of a basic and fairly unsophisticated, 'sophomore' level, and that more sophisticated models are just as likely to be misleading as helpful in real world advising.[53]

Anyhow, according to the President of the Royal Economic Society (1972), and also the Director of the National Institute, a significant amount of teaching in advanced economics is harmful or dangerous. There is 'feedback' evidence, according to Sir Henry Phelps Brown, which seems to support this view:

It may even be that training in advanced economics is actively unhelpful. I find it is a common experience that when graduates in economics first assume practical responsibilities they have something to unlearn. One lecturer in economics, latterly much concerned with international aid, has written to me, 'I find I've learnt a good deal in these last years – particularly how misleading most of my economic training has been. Apart from the basic tools of the trade, I find more and more that I draw on economic history rather than on anything in development theory.' An academically distinguished economist who has also had long experience in government service has told me, 'By far the best preparation for a useful career in economics after the university, is to go to an organisation working on practical problems, partly so as to understand how little use a great many of the academic gadgets are.'

Regarding the education of economists Sir Henry Phelps Brown calls for more history:

> It has long been agreed that the economist is not trained who is not numerate; but neither is he trained if he is not historiate.
>
> In the present stage of our science, at least, I believe that this relative valuation should be inverted: we ought to value powers of observation more highly than powers of abstraction, and the insight of the historian more than the rigour of the mathematician.[54]

Mr. Worswick sees as a danger the increasing concentration on mathematical techniques in the education of economists:

> The danger is that university courses in economics will become increasingly mathematical and increasingly concerned with technique to the exclusion of the subject matter itself. Such an imbalance is perhaps less dangerous for students going on to be professional economists than for those going on to posts in business or government. The former, when they do eventually come to try out their techniques on real problems, may learn to accept the constraints of the real world and adjust their methods accordingly, although one sees a disturbing amount of 'research' which is no more than exercising. But the latter, those going into government and business, finding such a large gap between what they have learned and the realities with which they are now confronted, may be inclined to dismiss all, and not merely some, of what they have learned as of no conceivable relevance to their future work. The more the impression is allowed to persist that economics is an exact science, or if not already one, then with the aid of mathematical models and the computer is about to become one, the more damage will be done to the subject when it fails to live up to exaggerated expectations.[55]

Finally, on the subject of the education of economists we may cite the views of Professor Kenneth Boulding (noting especially, perhaps, his point about how often 'quantification' involves abstraction). Though Professor Boulding is concerned with the rather different situation in the United States, his criticisms have much in common with those of Professor Phelps Brown when he deplores the 'anti-historical' emphasis in the contemporary education of economists:

The antihistorical method leads to the development of slick technicians who know how to use computers, run massive correlations and regressions, but who do not really know which side of anybody's bread is buttered, who are incredibly ignorant of the details of economic institutions, who have no sense at all of the blood, sweat and tears that have gone into the making of economics and very little sense of any reality which lies beyond their data. We seem to be producing a generation of economists whose main preoccupation consists of analyzing data which they have not collected and who have no interest whatever in what might be called a data-reality function, that is, into what extent a set of data corresponds to any significant reality in the world. The antihistorical approach, furthermore, leads to a rejection of any information which cannot easily be fitted onto punched cards or their equivalents, and hence results in a distortion of the information input in the direction of that which can easily be quantified and away from those intangibles and imponderables which may nevertheless be an essential part of reality. The antihistorical school, furthermore, leads into what I have called *Ptolemaic* economics, that is, an endless modification of variables and equations in regions of strongly diminishing returns in the knowledge function, and still sharper diminishing returns in the significance function. We seem to be engaged in finding out more and more numbers which mean less and less, and the parallel with the Ptolemaic epicycles is not difficult to draw.[56]

XI

It should be emphasised in conclusion that the crisis of abstraction is not the only kind of difficulty, or 'crisis', with which economics may be beset in the nineteen-seventies. There is also, for example, the related possibility of the increasing unpredictability of economic behaviour which we discussed in the chapter on 'Prediction and Economic Knowledge'. However, we may express the hope that the limitations of abstraction in economics, unrelated to historical cases, will become more clearly and widely recognised, and though we would hope, also, that a consequent marked trend towards a more empirical, historical and institutional emphasis will be forthcoming both in research and teaching, we are certainly not calling for a 'revolution'. Of much of existing, or 'orthodox' economics it can be said, as Churchill said of parliamentary democracy: it is full of faults, defects, inadequacies and disadvantages, but all the alternatives so far available are even more full of them, in some cases appallingly so. This is especially the case with regard to the vital form of knowledge which consists in a clear recognition of the extent of one's ignorance, about which 'Marxist' and 'radical' know-alls seem now to be even more glaringly defective than the so-called 'orthodox'.

Regarding what might be called (adapting one of Keynes's themes) 'The Possibilities of Economics for our Grandchildren', it does not seem that the fading away of economic problems is taking place in the way Keynes envisaged (1930), at any rate for much of the world. But what *might* indeed fade away, or perhaps disappear quite abruptly, is the free society, based on freedom of discussion and research. If this did disappear, economics, in any serious or interesting sense, would largely disappear too, except possibly for some accounting or statistical technicians. Though the natural sciences, or some of them, may survive, and in some ways flourish with the disappearance of a free society under a dictatorship, it seems very doubtful whether economics could survive. But if free societies are to continue, whether or not economics can do *very* much to bring about more successful economic policies, practitioners of the subject have a significant and seriously needed contribution to make in maintaining standards of free discussion, based at least on a modicum of free and rational argument and criticism, without which the free society itself will go under.

Five

Appendix: Economic Knowledge and Ignorance in Action: Economists on Devaluation and Europe, 1964-74

There exists a curious snobbery about the use of newspaper files and cuttings. The tolerance extended to a writer who employs them varies directly with the antiquity of the periodicals consulted. Thus if one is writing about early eighteenth-century politics, say, it is not only permissible but praiseworthy to quote from the press ('Shows a thorough knowledge of the pamphlet literature of the period'). The nineteenth century is slightly less safe. And to quote from the newspapers of the last ten years or so is to invite the charge of 'cuttings job' or 'scissors and paste'. Alan Watkins THE NEW STATESMAN AND NATION, 28 November, 1969.

I

Certainly to put together a record, from the resources available in newspaper files and cuttings – or from elsewhere – of the recent pronouncements by economists on economic policy, or aspects thereof, may be to risk manifestations of extreme displeasure from one or other economic 'establishment', or its PROS. But Mr. Watkins's diagnosis of 'snobbery' does not seem to provide the whole explanation so far as writings on economic policy are concerned. There are other reasons why an unduly frank, or insufficiently selective, record on this subject may seem tactless, indiscreet, or even (worst of all) 'unprofessional'.

Because although we may (and shall) be setting out many passages which display a full measure of subtle and discerning analysis and wise appraisal, while seeking to preserve a representative balance we shall also be citing passages which display just about the opposite of the foregoing qualities (from which it might be professionally more tactful simply to avert one's gaze). However, even *ex post facto*, there probably would not be much agreement as to which was which. For the record also reveals – and in recent years there have been quite fantastic illusions on this point – a width and depth of disagreement which, though inevitable, and even appropriate, given the nature of the material, may suggest a certain scepticism regarding ill-judged claims to economic expertise.

However, if one happens to be interested in questions of the nature of economic knowledge, and if one takes seriously the traditional, long-professed aims and claims of economists to provide guidance for real-world policies (aims and claims which are *very* seldom frankly renounced), then one cannot neglect, or attempt gallantly to laugh off, the kind of evidence forthcoming from 'cuttings jobs' or 'scissors and paste'. In fact those who try to dismiss or discount this material may be simply seeking to ward off *any* genuinely critical methodological appraisal of the record of economists' policy-pronouncements, by discrediting the basic empirical evidence which is available.[1]

For questions of what economists actually know, what they think they know, and what they don't know, may not only possess considerable epistemological and philosophical interest, they may have major political significance. For it is of some importance, for political contentedness and stability, that politicians and public should possess broadly realistic notions of what government economic policies can achieve. For this, a clear grasp is essential of the limits of economic knowledge and the extent of ignorance. For this, in turn, the record of economists' pronouncements on recent policy issues provides vital and indeed essential evidence. If false expectations, and subsequent dangerous disillusionment, are to be avoided in future, 'cuttings jobs' (for all the snobbery and outrage which they incur), which set out for examination what economists have said about recent policies, may have an essential role to play, quite apart from any more purely epistemological interest the contemplation of the extent and limits of economic knowledge may possess.

For the purposes of a case-study such as this, the question of devaluation presents as clearly and typically as any other the manifold problems of applying economic knowledge or 'theory' to the guidance of policy. First there is – or there is claimed to be – a body of relevant recognised exchange rate 'theory' or analysis to apply (which is hardly the case with such other major issues as growth policies or the 'right' level of aggregate demand). Secondly, though the devaluation question has various political angles and aspects, internal and external, which have frequently not been given their due weight in discussions by economists, attitudes to it have not been quite so thoroughly permeated and completely shaped, or polarised, by ideological presuppositions and bias, as in the cases of other leading policy issues (e.g. that of high *versus* low pressure of aggregate demand in running the economy). The devaluation issue to a large extent cuts across party lines and the usual ideological patterns. This means that differences of view over devaluation policy, though not much less wide and numerous than over other issues of economic policy, can, and to some extent actually do, turn rather more on questions of *relatively* unbiased, or less biased, positive economic predictions, and rather less on differing value-judgments and differing political biases. Not that these latter differences have been absent, but in considering the wide range of views on devaluation we shall be concerned with disagreements analysable *rather* more in terms of the varying economic judgment, than of the varying political or ideological tendencies, of the economists concerned. For example, experts with similar preferences for 'purposive' planning and for a very high pressure of demand and low level of unemployment, in some cases favoured devaluation and in others were highly sceptical. *Vice versa*, some of the most vigorous champions of free market policies were very sceptical of devaluation as a remedy for British difficulties, while others of the same general persuasion were early and enthusiastic advocates of devaluation.

It may be decades before a complete and reasonably reliable 'inside' history can be written of how the decisions, or non-decisions, came to be made by Ministers in the mid-sixties, and how they were influenced, or not influenced, by officials and advisers, though already various more or less inspired leaks have occurred, sometimes apparently, and perhaps misleadingly, slanted with the intention of establishing an alibi for particular individuals or groups. But quite a considerable and reasonably complete 'outside' story can be set in order with regard to the wide range of arguments of economists who committed themselves to public pronouncements on the question of the devaluation of the pound after 1963. Setting out such a record may at least nip some rapidly burgeoning myths in the bud.

However, we are more concerned with the material which such a survey provides regarding the basic methodological and practical questions of what economists know and how they know it, as contrasted with what they think or assume they know, and what, on the other hand, they don't know. For it could be maintained that if a proposition is to be regarded as a part of what economists know, it must be generally agreed by economists.[2]

The most obvious way of classifying opinions about devaluation is simply into 'For' and 'Against'. But this can only provide a rather rough first approach. More significant are the detailed questions of precise conditions and timing, and the nature and quality of the arguments brought forward on either side. At the two extremes there were, at the one end, those who seemed to be opposed to devaluation in almost any at all probable condition of the British economy, and, at the other end, there were facile or (as Sir Roy Harrod has called them) 'airy-fairy' devaluationists who seemed to regard devaluation as a certain and swift remedy, of negligible cost, in almost any circumstances, for almost any kind of balance-of-payments disequilibrium, which would lead to a rapid 'export-led' rise in the rate of growth up to that aspired to in the National Plan of 1965. In between, and towards the middle of the spectrum, disagreements centred more on questions of timing, or on differing judgments regarding conditions currently obtaining, inevitably difficult to assess or predict. For example, some economists seem to have held that, if the 'right' conditions could have been brought about, a devaluation of the pound was, or would have been, desirable at some earlier stage, but that the conditions were not in fact suitable until some time in 1967.

II

February 1963–July 1966

Devaluation began to be discussed in the early sixties in the context of the new concern with raising the rate of growth. It was put forward as a necessary or desirable means of protecting or improving the balance of payments when expansionist policies for growth, including as it was called 'the stopping of stop-go', got under way. For example, Mr. R. Neild (May 1961) and Professor R. C. Tress and Mr. J. M. Fleming (June 1962) suggested devaluation as providing 'a breathing space', or as a means of easing the balance-of-payments restraint on growth. The first significant public argument seems to have been that in *The Times* in February 1963 between Professor Kaldor, supported by Professor Day, urging devaluation, and, on the other side, Sir Roy Harrod and Dr. T. Balogh who were strongly and comprehensively opposed.[3] Regarding this exchange we simply wish to emphasise that, as then noted especially by Professor Day, *the case for devaluation was made at a time when spare capacity, as indicated by the unemployment percentage (then 3.9 per cent unadjusted) was at a peak.* But almost immediately after, from about the second quarter of 1963 onwards, unemployment began to fall markedly, reaching 1.9 per cent in March 1964, 1.5 per cent in October

1964, and by July 1966 an almost record peace-time low level of 1.1 per cent. It is in most cases not at all clear how far those who advocated devaluation during this period (mid 1963 to end of 1966) considered it likely to be successful with un-employment at well under 2 per cent, or whether it may perhaps have been assumed that devaluation would be accom-panied by very drastic deflationary measures making rapidly for spare capacity and raising unemployment up to, or well above, 2 per cent (though inevitably any such measures, how-ever drastic, would have needed some time to take effect).

During the pre-election boom period of 1964 the devaluation question received little attention, in public at any rate, though some strong opposition came in a pamphlet from the Royal Institute of International Affairs by Mr. C. W. McMahon:

> I believe that as things are the UK probably should never devalue. She might of course be driven to it by an over-whelming crisis: but it would be an act of desperation carrying no assurance that it would improve her situation. As a genuine, even if unlikely, alternative to other policies I do not think it has existed for the UK since about the middle of the 1950s. (The situation in 1949 was radically different, with extremely tight exchange controls operating in most countries and the European post-war recovery yet to begin.)
>
> This view is based, of course, on a belief as to where the UK's self-interest lies. I do not put it forward because I believe that the UK has a moral responsibility towards the holders of sterling or to uphold the world's payments system. That is simply speech-maker's cant. The obligations are in sterling not gold.[4]

It has several times been suggested that the Labour Govern-ment should have devalued immediately on taking office in October 1964 and it appears that the possibility may then have actually been discussed at the highest level. But in some cases these suggestions seem to have been made years after, in the light of clairvoyant hindsight, even by those who were quite

H

free to have urged devaluation publicly at the time. For those who allegedly considered the autumn of 1964 to be an appropriate time for devaluation as an obvious first step, an excellent opportunity for sounding off in the usual forum was provided in November when a general discussion of the balance-of-payments crisis broke out in *The Times*. Among the most vigorous contributions was one from two leading City financiers (Messrs. J. H. Hambro and S. G. Warburg) denouncing devaluation in the most extreme terms as both ineffective and immoral (21 November 1964).[5] We do not wish to emphasise this particular contribution so much as the very mild reaction to this challenge which was forthcoming in *The Times*. Among university economists only Dr. F. H. Hahn (30 November 1964) replied by calling for 'rational' discussion free of moral denunciations, while Dr. I. M. D. Little (24 November 1964), certainly not envisaging devaluation as an immediate first step, but simply as a long-term possibility, wrote in very cogently as follows:

I do not wish to argue that we ought to have devalued either a year ago, or this month, or that we should do so in the fairly near future...

We suggest that an important aim of long run policy is to get this country into a position in which it can change the value of its currency without violent political and moral objections being raised.

In the course of the same correspondence, the historian, Mr. Michael Hurst (19 December 1964), pertinently enquired (with unemployment at 1.5 per cent):

Is British industry at present able to exploit any sudden and large improvement in export prospects to the full? If not, surely devaluation of the pound sterling with the creation of such an improvement as its main attraction, would prove a superfluous and severely damaging measure to adopt just now?

It seems that only one university economist publicly suggested devaluation in the autumn of 1964.[8] This was Professor Alan Day. In *The Observer* (15 November 1964) he wrote:

My guess is that in 12 months' time Mr. Callaghan may regret that he did not listen to those who advised him that it would have been right (economically if not politically) to have a devaluation on coming into office, when it would have been justifiably easy to blame Tory improvidence.

A fortnight later (*Observer*, 29 November 1964) Professor Day maintained:

It is now perfectly clear to me that the Government made a first-rate error of judgment, when it decided not to devalue the pound during its first two or three weeks in power.

However, Professor Day (15 November) had considered Mr. Callaghan's emergency budget to be of 'the right kind' and noted the difficulty of imposing deflationary measures for a government with such an unqualified commitment to 'expansion' that it was unable initially to recognise that its predecessor had left it with a strongly inflationary legacy:

It must have been a little hard for a Government heavily committed to expansion to risk being accused of imposing another Stop.

Professor Day did not discuss the severity of the 'Stop' which would have been required for a successful devaluation with unemployment at about 1.5 per cent and falling, nor whether such measures could be expected from a government with a single-figure majority in the House of Commons.

By way of contrast with Professor Day's public commitment at the time, there is Mr. Opie's subsequent claim that for the new Labour Government in October 1964 devaluation was then '*the obvious first step*, as it seemed to most outsiders'. As regards the decision not to devalue Mr. Opie went on:

On economic grounds alone, the case for devaluation was
powerful, if not overwhelming. But the issue was decided on
political grounds. *This decision seemed, and still seems to me
a disastrous mistake.*[7]

But Mr. Opie only seems first to have publicly proclaimed
these views in an essay which appeared early *in 1968. What
Mr. Opie, as editor* of *The Bankers' Magazine, was actually
writing in December 1964 was*:

We believe that a devaluation of sterling at the present time
is neither the only nor the best solution to any of Britain's
economic problems. But one day it might be.[8]

In June 1965 Mr. Fred Hirsch's book *The Pound Sterling a
Polemic* appeared which vigorously argued for devaluation.
Regarding the role of the economists Mr. Hirsch maintained:

*Economists are nearly always divided on whether devaluation
is the appropriate remedy for a particular currency on a
particular occasion.* But, as noted above, they are not far from
unanimous in agreeing that such occasions can and do arise.[9]

Doubtless sufferers should feel gratified if medical scientists
were 'not far from unanimous' in agreeing that at least
occasions can and do arise when an operation for appendicitis
would be successful or beneficial. But the consolation might
prove somewhat tenuous for particular individual patients if
the experts were 'nearly always divided', *in any actual case,*
as to whether an operation should take place or not, because of
the particular condition of the patient, or the skill or lack of it
of the available surgeons. However, Mr. Hirsch certainly did
not minimise the rigours to be faced if success was to be
achieved:

The truth is that a successful devaluation is the reverse of a
soft option: it would have required a still *tougher* clamp-

down on consumer spending, on wages. In its first year the
policy would have been wildly unpopular. . . Doubtless
Mr. Wilson feared that a devaluation even on his very first
day in office after thirteen Tory years might still in the end
have confirmed Labour in the public mind as the party of
financial irresponsibility.[10]

Mr. Hirsch did not expect much from wage restraint, which
he saw as 'essentially a long-run aim' and as 'a weak and
hazardous instrument of trading adjustment'. At times he
seemed to imply that devaluation of itself 'promoted' the
necessary tough restraining measures *without* a determined,
strenuous effort by the Government perhaps far beyond its
political strength:

> The most powerful argument for devaluation is precisely
> that it does promote a tightening of belts by every family in
> the land, which is what getting out of balance of payments
> deficit is about.[11]

Mr. Hirsch interestingly examined the precedents, conceding
that 1949 had been less than successful for Britain, but claiming
success for Britain in 1931, France in 1958, and Canada in
1962. The question was how relevant these cases were to
Britain in 1965. In Britain in 1931 there had been over 20 per
cent unemployment. Regarding France in 1958:

> This was General de Gaulle's first year in office, and his
> national authority was strong. His domestic retrenchment
> actually produced a cut in real wages in 1959.[12]

There was also a sharp rise in unemployment. But Mr. Hirsch
did not explain whether he considered Mr. Wilson's political
position in 1965 to be remotely comparable with that of
de Gaulle in 1958 or whether anything like the same degree of
necessary tough retrenchment could have been expected from
the Labour Government with its single-figure majority and a
further election in prospect.

As regards Canada's devaluation of rather over 10 per cent to a fixed rate in 1962, Mr. Hirsch noted that, although unemployment had previously been at 6–7 per cent, the Government proceeded to cut its expenditure, while unemployment 'dropped below 5 per cent after devaluation'. Mr. Hirsch considered that economically the Canadian devaluation was a great success.[13] But he omitted to mention a political detail which might have been of some not illegitimate interest to Mr. Wilson: that the party whose Government had put through such an allegedly triumphantly successful and beneficial economic measure in May 1962 was beaten at the polls in April 1963 and was out of office for long afterwards. (Perhaps there were non-economic reasons for this defeat, but at least the Canadian Government does not seem to have benefited politically by a master-stroke of exchange-rate policy within a year of an election.)[14]

On the other hand, in 1965 opposition or scepticism was expressed by Professor R. Triffin in February.[15] In *The New Statesman* (9 July 1965, p. 36) whose whole record on devaluation is of some interest, Mr. Michael Posner, later to become Economic Adviser to the Treasury, argued forcefully against devaluation:

> This journal has never favoured devaluation. Its effect on real wages, on incomes and price policy, and on the hopes of a rational and orderly society, make it an inappropriate instrument – particularly for a Labour Government. . .
> But if the choice is inescapable, we would prefer to abandon the pound rather than to impose another three or four years' stagnation on the economy. Fortunately, it is not too late to avoid this choice. Mr. Wilson can impose his authority and protect the pound.

The National Institute of Economic and Social Research was perhaps somewhat inhibited by its para-official position in setting out arguments in favour of devaluation. Nevertheless the only arguments which it did present on the subject at this juncture were strongly *against* devaluation, though it was somewhat exaggerated for *The Times* to claim (20 August 1965) regarding the August issue of its *Review*, that 'the National Institute on this occasion comes out flatly against devaluation'. What the National Institute then emphasised was:

> Devaluation would make it even more difficult to get prices and money incomes under control, so that any favourable effects on the balance of payments might rather quickly be eroded by intensified inflation.[16]

An interesting review of the arguments came in September 1965 in Professor Coppock's article 'The Alleged Case against Devaluation'. With due academic restraint Professor Coppock claimed that his analysis was 'mainly one of principle' and went on:

> I make no claim to precise knowledge of the quantitative effects of a given devaluation on the UK balance of payments, whether in the short run or the longer run. But no one else, as far as I am aware, knows the precise answers to these interesting questions either. What the academic observer can do is to point out contradictions or errors of reasoning, in particular those of practical men who are apt to dogmatise on a basis of personal experience even though they may be ignorant of the theoretical issues involved. Similarly, it is not for me to suggest the size or timing of the devaluation even if such a policy were judged appropriate.[17]

But if an academic, or anyone else, can only discuss the issue in non-quantitative terms of 'principle', with no precise quantitative estimates, *it might seem, perhaps, that he could go little further in terms of support than to throw out the question, when balance-of-payments difficulties arise, of 'What about devaluation?'* Actually, after an inevitably rather impressionistic analysis of the relevant elasticities, Professor Coppock was

prepared on that basis to offer the 'presumption that devaluation would be successful'. However, Professor Coppock (p. 305)
warned:

> A UK devaluation, if not to prove abortive, would have to be
> associated with measures to limit severely the defensive
> reactions of the unions.

He added (p. 309) the significant suggestion:

> There would be a good case for allowing a measure of output
> deflation to precede an actual devaluation in order to limit
> the destructive reactions to it.

But Professor Coppock did not offer any estimate of *how much*
deflation – and unemployment – might be necessary and for
how long, and against what political pressures, it might have
to be maintained, if the devaluation was not to prove 'abortive'.
Finally Professor Coppock (p. 309) suggested:

> If sterling had been devalued in 1963 as an alternative to the
> expansionary measures of the 1963 Budget ... the UK might
> now be experiencing a period of export-led growth instead
> of the present stagnation and uncertainty, with almost
> ludicrous flurries of optimism and pessimism as each
> successive set of monthly trade or reserve figures is released,
> complete with misleading random components.

In the early months of 1966 there was some further support
for devaluation, quite enthusiastic in the case of Mr. J. H.
Williamson,[18] though somewhat hesitant in a symposium on
the British Balance of Payments in *The Scottish Journal of
Political Economy* (February 1966). Here Professor J. R.
Parkinson, estimating as high as 5 the long-term elasticity of
demand for British exports, maintained that 'price is likely to
be an even more important determinant of export sales'. But
he considered that the opportunity had passed:

The opportunity to devalue comfortably by a moderate amount and before having to undertake borrowing on a large scale is now over. It was not an unjustifiable decision to refrain from devaluation provided that suitable policies to improve competitiveness of our exports could be made effective.

In the same symposium Mr. P. M. Oppenheimer took a rather resigned view but perceptively noted the importance of 'electoral considerations':

The sense of obligation to the sterling area and concern that the dollar (and hence other major currencies) might be forced to follow a change in the sterling parity have helped to rule out devaluation in the 1960s. This is unfortunate, as there has been a strong case for devaluing on general economic grounds. But the sterling problem cannot be held solely responsible; electoral considerations too have militated against devaluation.

The editor, Professor D. J. Robertson, concluded rather unenthusiastically:

Few believe that devaluation alone would help the British balance of payments in any permanent way, though some may feel that a price advantage would be immediately beneficial.[19]

Further scepticism came from Professor D. C. Rowan, editor of *The Bankers' Magazine* (February 1966, p. 124), who maintained:

A devaluation seems highly unlikely, at least in the immediate future: the authorities still have quite substantial reserves to defend the parity while, moreover, a devaluation would do little to cure the country's problems which stem, at least in part, from large-scale imports of capital equipment.[20]

From early in 1963 pre-election manoeuvring and, naturally, the promotion and maintenance of boom conditions, dominated policies. Owing to the inconclusive result of the last-minute election in October 1964 these political conditions continued right through until April 1966. Whether anything like the prerequisites necessary for the success of devaluation could have been sustained in such conditions seems doubtful, even if either government might otherwise have been prepared seriously to consider such a decision. The politics of devaluation required, in the opinion of the time, a readiness to face both an immediate unfavourable psychological impact effect in terms of heightened anxieties and loss of prestige (or what was believed to be such) and also the unpopularities of a medium – or longer-term – restraint, or 'slog' if lasting benefits are to be achieved. If economic policy proposals are to amount to something more than abstract speculations at least *some* slight account must be taken of the political facts of life in an electoral democracy. Economically, with a roaring boom, a rapidly worsening balance of payments, and unemployment at 1.5 per cent and falling, it might well have required an all-time record in deflationary 'stop' packages if devaluation in the winter of 1964–5 was not to have ended in disastrous failure. On the other hand the wave of fashionable expansionist *mystique*, on which the Government had attained office, was one of 'riding out' or 'driving through' balance-of-payments deficits, of 'stopping stop-go', 'burying Selwyn Lloyd' and 'nailing him down in his coffin', that is, one of 'Balance of Payments through Joy' as Professor R. J. Ball has well described it. In fact impatient and dogmatic expansionism and the pursuit of over-full employment and 'dashes for growth' probably rule out any lastingly effective devaluation. So obsessed with this *mystique* were the new government's economic policy-makers that they quite failed to appreciate the seriousness of the over-heating of the economy stimulated by their predecessors.[21] By proclaiming that it would run the economy without resorting to deflationary 'stops' the Government left itself incapable of recognising or adequately criticising the electorally motivated expansionism of its predecessor. In fact the new Government's commitment to expansionism, and its social priorities, were scarcely reconcilable with the restraints necessary *if* devaluation was to have been successful for the British economy. Moreover high hopes were being held out at that time that rising costs would be restrained by what was described as 'the planned growth of incomes'.[22] But some economists believed that devaluation was a method of righting Britain's balance of payments at negligible costs in restraint, deflation, or unemployment, and of fulfilling the ambitious growth targets in the National Plan of 1965.

III

July 1966–November 1967

The decisive election result of 31 March 1966 transformed the political, but not the economic, situation. A large element in the party-political case against devaluation, important in and after October 1964, had now lost most of its weight. The Government now had an effective majority with nearly five years of power in front of it. The apparently quite unforeseen crisis of July was the next major event. It may well be that as a result of that traumatic crisis an increasing number of economists began to move in favour of devaluation. But although the previous political restraints had disappeared, unemployment was at an almost record low level of 1.1 per cent. Anyhow, three eminent authorities, of widely differing political standpoints, and differing priorities regarding levels of unemployment, came out in opposition to devaluation in the second half of 1966. One, Sir John Hicks, expressed forthright opposition to what he called 'the favourite remedy' and congratulated the Prime Minister:

> It is widely supposed that the only reason why we do not devalue is the obstinacy of Mr. Wilson. But economists may be grateful for the obstinacy of Mr. Wilson and for the good

advice on this matter we may be sure he is receiving. . . There is really no alternative while our position is so weak but to cling to the existing parity.[23]

Secondly, Professor Joan Robinson, holding that allowing unemployment to rise above 2 per cent would be 'cold-blooded' and 'out of the question', expressed much scepticism about devaluation in conditions of near-full employment:

> In a situation where there is some unemployment and unused
> capacity in many lines, a devaluation increases activity and
> improves the balance of trade at one stroke. But when there
> is near-full employment already it is liable merely to increase
> the pressure of demand for labour, while the rise in price of
> imports increases the pressure for higher money-wage rates,
> so that before long the competitive advantage of lower home
> costs is completely lost.[24]

Thirdly, Lord Robbins in the House of Lords, though certainly not sharing Professor Robinson's absolute priority for keeping unemployment under 2 per cent, also expressed his strong opposition to devaluation:

> I welcome greatly the declaration . . . expressing the firm
> decision of the Government not to resort to this expedient.
> I do not think indeed that in present circumstances this view
> that we should have devalued has much practical applic-
> ability.[25]

Lord Robbins added that he did not rule out devaluation in all circumstances but emphasised the dangers when 'the level of unemployment is almost at an all-time record low for peace-time'.

On the other hand, vigorous advocacy of devaluation came from Mr. R. Pryke who, almost immediately after taking up a post in the Cabinet office, resigned in protest against the measures of July 1966 and the failure to devalue. Certainly

Mr. Pryke allowed that if the Government 'had devalued it would have had to take firm action to restrict home demand'. Mr. Pryke seemed very close to Professor Joan Robinson with regard to the overriding priority for keeping unemployment under 2 per cent, but he argued optimistically that, with devaluation, such sufficiently 'firm action' would not have caused any appreciable rise in unemployment:

> Little unemployment is, however, likely to occur. Most firms sell in both home and foreign markets and as the pressure of domestic demand falls the slack will be taken up by the rise in export demand due to devaluation. Firms will therefore have no need to lay off workers and *redeployment of labour will occur automatically and painlessly as production switches from home to export markets*. Here again there is a sharp contrast between the consequences of devaluation and deflation. With devaluation there is little unemployment but large-scale redeployment; with deflation there is large-scale unemployment but very little redeployment.[26]

Perhaps this general qualitative contrast was somewhat overdrawn. Anyhow, Mr. Pryke did not precisely indicate how much the 'little' unemployment would have amounted to, and for how long it might have been required if devaluation was to be successful. As we have noted, in July 1966, unemployment was at a level of 1.1 per cent (unadjusted) which was almost a peace-time record. Mr. Pryke might be understood to be suggesting that considerably less unemployment would have been necessary for an effective devaluation than in fact came about over the next six to twelve months as a result of the deflationary measures of July 1966. Nevertheless, Mr. Pryke certainly expressed the strongest aversion to any significant rise in unemployment:

> If nothing is done unemployment may rise higher than it did during the Conservatives' deflationary bout... For a Labour Government deliberately to throw men out of work must

rank as one of the great betrayals of principle by a political party.[27]

Meanwhile, in *The New Statesman* (29 July 1966) an expert described as 'Our Economic Correspondent' opposed devaluation on three grounds (all slightly dubious):

> What then should be done? One of the reasons for rejecting devaluation is that, to make it work, deflation would have been necessary. We now have deflation: why not devalue? For various reasons we do not believe that this is a real possibility at the moment – partly because of the technical state of the Bank of England's dealings, partly because foreign repercussions must be such as to make the exercise nugatory, partly because of Mr. Wilson's commitment not to. Economics, like politics, is the art of the possible.

It was only in the latter part of 1966 that unemployment began to rise appreciably, not passing 2 per cent (seasonally adjusted) until the opening months of 1967. In March *The New Statesman* at last published an isolated article in favour of devaluation by Mr. R. Marris, who explained his reasons for having opposed devaluation until then:

> I have personally hesitated to advocate devaluation openly mainly because there have been very considerable obstacles to a successful adjustment of sterling throughout almost the whole period since the end of 1964.

Perhaps the obstacles went back to well before October 1964. Anyhow, Mr. Marris explicitly argued, against Mr. Pryke, that devaluation in the circumstances of the previous July would have been most disadvantageous:

> Mr. Pryke believes that we should have devalued last July, but this might have had all the political and economic drawbacks of devaluation from weakness.[28]

We have noted that Sir Roy Harrod had strongly opposed devaluation back in 1963. He had indeed criticised the 1949 devaluation from about 1950 onwards, and was to continue his criticism and opposition after that of November 1967. In some lectures published in 1967 Sir Roy referred to devaluation as 'entirely ruled out for valid reasons' and as

the most potent known instrument of domestic price inflation, which has such sorry effects on human welfare.[29]

In April 1967 very able and sensible presentations of the cases for and against were undertaken in *The Bankers' Magazine* by Mr. M. F. Scott and Professor R. J. Ball.[30] Mr. Scott conceded modestly that he could not 'claim to know enough to give this very serious problem the treatment it deserves'. He admitted:

A decision to devalue now would be hard to take and, in political terms, perhaps harder to defend than the alternative of maintaining the existing rate of exchange, especially since the immediate outlook for the balance of payments is good.

On the other hand:

The present moment is particularly opportune since, with unemployment rising and more slack in the economy, we are in a better position to take advantage of a devaluation than for some years.

Mr. Scott feared that if the Government was 'unlucky so far as the balance of payments is concerned' it might be driven to impose import restrictions, which would 'bring a serious danger of retaliation'. He estimated that a devaluation of 10 per cent would bring an improvement in the balance of payments of the order of £300 or £400 million after a year or so. But Mr. Scott admitted that objections to devaluation 'have some force', notably those that it made prices rise faster and that it might encourage further speculation against the pound. He conceded also that reluctance to devalue based simply on the fear of the unknown was 'not entirely irrational' and predicted that 'the pound will almost certainly not be devalued in the near future'.

Professor R. J. Ball, on the other hand, expressed determined opposition. Declaring himself 'a devaluation pessimist', he criticised the grounds on which some economists seemed to be supporting devaluation:

> To argue for devaluation simply to avoid the unpleasant consequences of alternatives may also be irrational. In particular there is certainly a feeling abroad that anything is better than deflation, so that devaluation obtains support not on the economic merits of the case but because any device to avoid some unemployment is worth trying. To devalue on these grounds would be to take a dangerously short term view... The danger is that it may not be realised that a successful devaluation itself imposes a cost that the community must be prepared to bear if success is to be achieved.

In fact Professor Ball went further than most opponents of devaluation in expressing disbelief in the simple effectiveness of price factors and elasticities of demand for exports, about which other economists had been highly optimistic:

> I believe that the non-price factors and the approach to marketing as a whole, together with the capacity problem, lie at the heart of the long term trend, and that the problem of price is by no means the most significant factor that enters into the Balance of Payments equation... *Even if the once and for all effect of a single change did provide a surplus on current account rapidly and of the right order of magnitude, we have done nothing to ensure that when long run growth and expansion is resumed our position will not further be eroded.* The result could be the need for yet another devaluation... The most optimistic view of devaluation that I feel able to take is that it might provide a breathing space.[31]

On 20 July 1967, at a Conservative Party Economic Seminar, three economists (Messrs. M. J. Farrell, G. Pyatt, and especially S. Brittan) supported devaluation, while three others (Messrs. G. D. N. Worswick, R. J. Ball and P. Bareau) were at least decidedly unenthusiastic, or, in the case of the two last-named, strongly opposed. Mr. Brittan's plea seemed to sound a note of near-desperation:

Whether one is keen on changing the exchange rate or reluctant, whether one is impressed by the arguments for devaluation or not is almost irrelevant. The onus is on the other side. What matters is to look at everything that is being inflicted on us, to preserve the exchange rate and ask if the price is worth paying.[32]

On the other hand Mr. Worswick set out the issue in rather noncommittal but sceptical terms:

It is admitted that devaluation will worsen the terms of trade, that is to say we should have to give even more exports than before per unit of desired imports. But the supply of these extra exports will be forthcoming from the slack to be taken up and the accelerated growth of output. But what if you don't think that there is much pressure in this spring, then you will have serious doubts about devaluation. Not on the grounds that it won't make your exports cheaper to the foreigner, of course it will, but about your capacity to generate them on the required scale. And in that case you would attack the problem from the other side as it were, and advocate the restriction of imports (p. 5).

Professor R. J. Ball restated some of the arguments of his April paper. He commented critically on the mood in which devaluation was increasingly being advocated:

I think it is without doubt the case that devaluation is the solution favoured by the majority of economists. I have the

I

impression that for many . . . devaluation is in fact the last council of despair partly on the grounds that anything is worth trying rather than deflation. As one leading American economist put it to me recently – 'What is there left, in fact, except to devalue?'

Perhaps the most vehement opposition came from Mr. Paul Bareau, though he considered justifiable the devaluations of 1931 and 1949:

I am no believer in the fact that an exchange rate is always sacrosanct. If a currency is over-valued, is really over-valued, then obviously it ought to be devalued. . . But today – no! Sterling is not over-valued. We are not being priced out of world markets. The real reason for our balance of payments difficulties is . . . the overseas expenditure of the Government which seems to grow with every diminution of the overseas responsibilities of the Government. Basically it is also a national attitude – the national attitude to innovation, to honest work, to the pursuit of exports, to intelligent management. . . Devaluation in these circumstances would do precisely the reverse of what ought to be done. It would make life just tolerable for the inefficient. It would remove the spur, the urgency for making the really fundamental reforms that ought to be made, and that will have to be made – it would, in fact be a disaster for Britain; it would be equivalent to drug taking.

Mr. Bareau further emphasised the cost to sterling and to London as an international financial centre, the 'incitement to inflation', and the cost in terms of honesty involved in 'bilking on part of your debt'.

IV

November 1967–November 1969

On 17 November 1967, the day before devaluation was actually announced, Mr. R. Opie argued strongly in favour in *The New Statesman*. But he proceeded to castigate Mr. Maudling for holding that further deflationary measures would be necessary if devaluation was to be effective:

> Mr. Maudling had his own theory as well – those 'who think devaluation is an alternative to deflation are totally wrong'. *If Mr. Maudling is right, every textbook will have to be re-written. He even seems to think that 'the only way of making devaluation effective would be to have even tougher deflation'.* When there is more than £1 billion of excess capacity already?[33]

However, a week later, after the announcement, Mr. Opie was jubilant. He began:

> On 16 October 1964, the Labour government won office. *On 18 November 1967, it won power.* This is the proper measure of what has been achieved by devaluation. . . It was a copy-book performance. It was a devaluation of the right amount *made in the right economic conditions accompanied by the right supporting measures.* It was shown to be the right amount in that none of our competitors – the industrialised exporters – has retaliated.

Mr. Opie noted, however, one 'puzzling' feature:

> It is a puzzling paradox that devaluation has to be accompanied in any highly-employed (even if not fully-employed) economy, by deflation.

Mr. Opie concluded:

This is not just the old stick of deflation – it is a combination
of stick at home *and* carrot abroad. *It must work*. . . It will
then be essential to avoid becoming the Brazil of Europe, and
find ourselves forced to devalue again. If we can avoid that
danger we will at last achieve export-led growth – *and the
British economic miracle will succeed those other miracles
we have envied so much.*[34]

Professor Day, on the other hand, regarded devaluation as
'a magnificent opportunity', but warned that it might be used
for other purposes than improving the balance of payments and
the condition of the British economy:

There is, however, a real risk that devaluation will be taken
not as an opportunity to get the economy into a prosperous
and stable state, but simply to make sure that Mr. Wilson is
still Prime Minister in the early 1970s. . . There is need for
an intellectual astringency which has been sadly lacking in
the Government's policies.[35]

One might add that it was not simply in the Government's
policies that 'intellectual astringency' had been lacking. There
seems, however, to have been wide agreement that further
severely restrictive measures were necessary following on the
forced devaluation, although unemployment then was well
over 2 per cent. Indeed there was some criticism of the Government for the delay in bringing them forward. But it is note-
worthy that even so comparatively cautious and sophisticated a
supporter of devaluation, as the Chancellor might be described,
hesitated before introducing his deflationary package. However,
we might note here, on the other side, that Sir Roy Harrod,
though he was, of course, opposed to 'the unfortunate devaluation', continued in a letter to *The Times* (21 December 1967)
with his advocacy of extreme expansionist views and rising
consumption:

I find quite the wrong idea present in the minds of those of
most political complexions – namely, that we now have to

brace ourselves to a period of grim austerity. . . On the contrary what we need now is industrial expansion. *It is idle to suppose that we can have an expanding economy on the basis of more exports and more 'investment' only; we need rising consumption also. . . To ensure that the unfortunate devaluation, entailing a rise in prices, does not reduce standards of living, taxes should be reduced*; the Budget surplus is now unnecessarily high. . . I am convinced that the idea that austerity is an appropriate remedy for our troubles has been the most important cause of them in recent times.

Sir Roy added that our citizens 'must give up their insensate preference for foreign goods and buy British'. But Sir Roy's, always rather an extreme, was, for the moment, a somewhat lone voice in advocating expansion. For a short time – but only for a short time – after devaluation there was something of a truce in the perennial battle, largely ideological, between advocates of a high *versus* a low pressure of aggregate demand.[36] The Chancellor's record deflationary budget of March 1968 was fairly generally accepted, and indeed widely applauded. Professor Day, who found the 'cuts' in Government expenditure in January to be 'inadequate' and 'profoundly disappointing', awarded the Budget, two months later, 'top marks'.

In a volume from Manchester completed in April 1968 on *The U.K. Economy* a more pessimistic view regarding devaluation prospects was balanced by a more optimistic one. Mr. N. J. Gibson confessed:

The response is to a degree unpredictable as exports depend heavily on events in the rest of the world, particularly the level of economic activity. Imports, on the other hand, are greatly affected by domestic policy. For what it is worth this writer expects further balance of payments crises, given a serious commitment to such policy goals as a fixed, or at any rate temporarily fixed exchange rate, full employment, rapid economic growth and some more freedom of action, for the individual members of the community in economic matters.

Professor D. J. Coppock, on the other hand, though somewhat cautious and reserved, seemed, on balance, to be more hopeful:

The major necessary condition for a return to equilibrium has been taken and the problem of policy is now one of implementing successfully the supporting measures which are required to make the devaluation effective.

Professor Coppock went on:

It cannot be emphasised too much that the potential gains to the balance of payments from devaluation will not be realised unless the government takes measures to release resources from domestic use to make room for the expansion of exports and import substitutes. The extent to which this point has been stressed in discussion in Parliament and the press is a welcome sign that the full implications of devaluation, as a policy, are now much better understood. The principle is clear, but exact computation of the required cuts in domestic expenditure is made difficult in practice since it is not easy to predict the size and phasing of the potential demand on resources. Although unemployment was relatively high at the time of devaluation *the margin of excess capacity was too small to dispense with resource-releasing policies.*[37]

Professor Coppock considered it unlikely that 'the aim will be achieved on the basis of a purely voluntary prices and incomes policy', though he maintained that 'if opinion were sampled among professional economists we should probably find a majority view that devaluation came several years too late'.

In the early summer of 1968 optimism continued to prevail, though it was reasonably cautious optimism in the case of Professor Day who warned that 'the situation is still sufficiently delicate for an inflationary boom to wreck everything'. What the Chancellor needed, according to Professor Day (*Observer*, 19 May 1968), is a clear fall in consumer demand. . .

Only by keeping the clamp on tight can we hope to break through from the present initial signs that the payments problem is being solved to a position where everyone can plainly see that it has been overcome.

A week later Professor Day added: 'No reduction in unemployment can be safely tolerated until exports really are roaring away.' However:

The Government does have an economic strategy which, given sufficient time, promises far better chances of success than any alternative that can be dreamed up.[38]

Mr. Opie continued highly optimistic. In *The New Statesman* (14 June 1968) he affirmed: 'I believe that the end of the tunnel is at last in sight.'

By November, however, further measures necessary for 'keeping the clamp on tight', as Professor Day had considered essential, were under discussion.[39] Mr. Opie expressed much alarm, calling as a 'last hope' for the retirement of Mr. Jenkins and for a pre-election boom on the 'you-never-had-it-so-good' lines of 1959: jobs were at stake: the Government's electoral chances were being jeopardised:

After four years of virtually non-stop squeeze, another turn of the screw – tighter bank credit, or HP restrictions, or perhaps an increase in indirect tax rates – is rumoured. If it happens, it will be the last confession of bankrupt management. It will also be a strange reaction to the miracle the PM managed to discern in the early summer – *indeed one's last hope may yet be that, like Macmillan, who sensed his government's recovery from a similar trough of demoralised gloom in early 1958 and stamped on the deflationary absurdities of Thorneycroft, Harold Wilson will do the same 10 years later. . . To squeeze now would be nothing short of economic madness.*[40]

However, HP restrictions were duly tightened a day or two later, while in the next fortnight, following the franc–mark crisis, plans for the sharp use of the regulator were implemented to increase indirect taxes, while a scheme for import deposits was introduced. Professor Day concluded (*Observer*, 24 November) that it was

> quite clear, even before last week's events, that further tax increases and a tightening of bank lending were necessary and on the way. Roughly speaking, about half the present measures, or rather more, could have been expected anyway if there had been no international crisis.

In fact money and credit conditions continued to be tightened and bank rate was raised to 8 per cent the following February. But the 'hard slog', with nothing so far to show for it, was beginning to be found rather tiresome in some quarters, and with the election approaching over the horizon the brief truce observed by expansionists was showing signs of erosion. There were murmurings about a possible further devaluation or a floating of the pound. Professor Alan Day in a review of the possibilities maintained that another devaluation would politically

> be an even more effective form of suicide for the Prime Minister than the others facing him, which makes it highly unlikely to be adopted.[41]

Professor Day concluded that 'soldiering on', which the Government clearly intended doing, was the course which 'makes the most sense both economically and politically over the next few months'.

In June, however, came the first faint indications of a turning-point, along with the episode of the 'lost' exports, rediscovered by the Board of Trade's statisticians (which showed how uncertain was the statistical basis for policy-making and argumentation). Mr. Robin Marris in an article entitled 'The Great Export Scandal' maintained:

Until about the middle of the present decade many critics such as myself argued that the UK's troubles mainly arose from the existence of the sterling balances plus a long-term capital outflow. Events after the beginning of 1964, however, convinced us that the current balance was also chronically unhealthy, and eventually led us to recommend devaluation. The new export figures do not change that view, because there were so many general signs of weakness and the balance revealed remains rather precarious. All this said, *one now faces the startling fact that from the end of 1964 to Devaluation Day (18 November 1967), the new figures show the Labour Government had no cumulative deficit on current account – rather an almost exact balance.*[42]

Mr. Marris argued:

Clearly, if the true figures had been known, it might have been even more difficult to persuade Messrs. Wilson and Callaghan to undertake a planned devaluation from moderate strength in early 1967.

He concluded

A planned, properly timed devaluation is a difficult trick to achieve, but it was never tried.

Again the trade figures swung back unfavourably and in August the French devaluation caused further forebodings. But at last, in September – with unforeseen suddenness – came an unambiguously favourable swing in the balance of visible trade which continued until the end of the year and into 1970.

In the next year or two no decisive verdict seemed to emerge. Certainly the more optimistic visions soon faded away, such as, for example, that devaluation would enable growth targets like those in the National Plan of 1965 to be realised, or that it would give us

room for manoeuvre for years to come . . . enabling British

governments for the first time since 1952, to ignore the
balance of payments in their growth policies.[43]

Mr. Peter Jay maintained:

It is, however, obvious enough that devaluation and
subsequent Government strategy has not yet and in all
probability will never accomplish that decisive departure
from Britain's economic travails which is needed.[44]

Mr. Jay now called for more flexibility or a 'crawling peg'
for the pound. Mr. Samuel Brittan, another erstwhile enthusiast,
concluded:

Even two years after devaluation, there must still be an
element of agnosticism in one's appraisal.[45]

But he maintained that the British authorities

are better placed – although they do not quite realise it
themselves – to deal with any fresh payments shocks in the
1970s than they were in the 1960s...

We are not attempting here to follow closely the record from
1970 onwards on the subject of devaluation and a flexible or
floating exchange rate – which was one of the next main
'talking points'. But one major conflict of views which subsequently emerged may be noted. We have cited above the strong
opposition, which soon began to develop, to the restrictive
policies of Mr. Jenkins and his 'two years' hard slog' following
the 1967 devaluation. This opposition was expressed especially
stridently in *The New Statesman* by Mr. R. Opie, who described
the budget of 1970 as 'flat, stale and unprofitable', in that
Mr. Jenkins had rejected 'a real opportunity to break out of the
cycle in his last budget'. Mr. Opie complained that the Wilson
government had made a new definition of full employment –
'only' 2–2½ per cent unemployed – respectable. He urged:

If the present wage explosion is to be continued without pushing up wage costs, and prices steadied without pushing up profit margins, *demand must be expanded*.[46]

However, by early 1974 the whole approach represented by these criticisms of Mr. Jenkins was being denounced, again in *The New Statesman*, by Lord Kaldor, who demanded the rejection of the economics of what soon came to be called 'the conventional post-war demand-management school', which upheld what Lord Kaldor described as 'the accustomed ways of thinking of enlightened opinion'.

On the other hand, Lord Kaldor confidently proclaimed himself '*sure*' that Britain's unsuccessful economic performance since the war

does not lie in some deep-seated defect in the ability or motivation of the British business manager. The true explanation, in my view, lies in a more mundane field: in the techniques of economic management developed in this country during and after the war and followed, on official advice, by successive governments, both Conservative and Labour.[47]

But the correct and most up-to-date fiscal-managerial expertise was essential, and Lord Kaldor proceeded to denounce the kind of policies advocated by his fellow *New Statesman* contributor Mr. Opie, and in particular the idea of

bold Keynesian policies of expansion which, if pursued long enough and consistently enough and undeterred by short-run balance of payments obstacles, should finally lead to a productivity breakthrough that would align Britain with the more successful European countries.

If the 'conventional' errors (so recently, so long, and so aggressively proclaimed in *The New Statesman*) were abandoned, then – Lord Kaldor reassuringly asserted – in order to break out of the stop-go cycle of low growth, there *was* an alternative strategy which, had it been followed, could have led us on to the path of self-sustaining and rapid growth to which ever since the war all political parties have aspired.

According to Lord Kaldor, the successful growth of exports which was achieved in 1960–70 was

thanks not only to the improved competitiveness, *but to Mr. Jenkins' Budgets which provided the resources for the rise in exports.*[48]

This praise covers, obviously, the measures denounced by Mr. Opie as 'nothing short of economic madness', in November 1968.

However, the opportunity provided by Mr. Jenkins' courageous budgets was thrown away, according to Lord Kaldor, by

Mr. Barber's policy of counteracting the tendency to recession by large injections of money to bolster up consumer demand ... and of expanding domestic demand through lower taxation, higher public expenditure and easy credit.

Of course, contrasts and contradictions such as those between Lord Kaldor's views and those of his predecessors in *The New Statesman* are inevitable, given the extremely complex, shifting, uncertain nature of the subject-matter. What is wrong is not that such contrasts and contradictions occur from time to time, but the kind of claims to 'expertise' based on a failure to grasp the nature of economic knowledge and ignorance, together with the overconfident rejection, as equivalent to 'flat-earth' beliefs, of points of view which clashed with the particular nostrum currently in fashion.

V

At this point attention should be called to the development of a myth or fantasy regarding economists' views on devaluation which arose out of the involvement of the devaluation issue with the defence of the economic record of the Labour Government from 1964 to 1970. We have an illustration here of how the history of economic thought and opinion may often originate in polemical, and more or less political, attempts at self-justification.

The Labour record was perhaps not so *very* much below the average of British governments in the previous half-century. The novel feature which imparted some piquancy to its examination was that in 1964 a throng of university economists (or 'expert manpower', as Mr. Opie described it)[49] moved into Whitehall on a scale unprecedented in peace-time. This movement took place to the accompaniment of denunciations of previous mismanagement of economic policy by 'dilettantes', and of proclamations that, with the aid of this expert manpower, 'stop-go' would be stopped, the growth rate raised to nearer 5–5½ per cent than 4 per cent, and a National Plan launched with an incomes policy for which the support of the trade unions was soon claimed.[50] Perhaps a much larger contribution was made to very serious political disillusion by the stimulation of extravagant expectations than by the mediocre level of the actual record.[51] Anyhow after 1970 an urgent need was obviously felt for some kind of myth, explanation, or alibi, to explain the yawning gap between promises and performance.

According to the myth, all sensible people, or all, or almost all, economists, were in favour of devaluation, if not by October 1964, when Labour took office, at any rate by 1965 or July 1966. (It may be noted that the myth was *not* simply asserted that *from the beginning of 1967 onwards* there was a considerable increase in support for devaluation – which *might* have had some truth.) According to the myth, the expert advice of the economists was rejected by a plague of 'politicians', or some sinister 'sterling-first lobby' in the Treasury and the Bank[52] (though one of the main citadels of anti-devaluation dogmas was certainly *The New Statesman*). This political rejection of a unanimous, or almost unanimous expert consensus on devaluation inevitably brought about, and therefore excused, the wide range of failures in the economic field or 'the poverty of the government's performance' as Mr. Opie described it.[53]

We are simply concerned here with the myth or fantasy about the opinions of economists, not with the substantive issue as to the effects of an earlier devaluation between 1964 and 1967. We are certainly not concerned to deny that at that juncture a beneficial devaluation might possibly have been achieved by an omniscient and temporarily omnipotent philosopher-statesman, who did not care whether or not he was going to be re-elected to his office after his term had expired.

The myth was conveyed in statements such as the following (almost entirely devoid of factual foundation):

> By October 1964 many ... economists ... were convinced that the balance of payments problem could not be solved except by devaluation. *By July 1966 this opinion must have been virtually unanimous.*[54]

Again, apparently on the basis of inside information it was stated:

> *The vast majority of economists,* including the Government's senior advisers, agreed *by early 1965* that devaluation was needed if Britain was to secure external balance without large-scale unemployment.[55]

Later it was maintained that

> by *early 1966* there was probably *hardly an economist in the country* who did not advocate devaluation.[56]

Then again it was asserted:

By the time the Labour Government was elected *there could
hardly have been a sensible person in the country* who did not
think that devaluation was both desirable and inevitable.[57]

We are not concerned here with the political motivation and
implications of this myth, which relates to the apportionment,
as between politicians and economic experts, of responsibility
for the economic record of the Labour government (1964–70).[58]
But such sheer gratuitous inventiveness does deserve recognition. It may be wondered how far this inventiveness has free
play over the whole range of factual material and empirical
'assumptions' in economics, or whether it enjoys an especial
freedom only with regard to economists' claims about their
colleagues' opinions, or the recent or contemporary history of
economic thought. Moreover, since the English classicals, there
have been repeated claims by economists as to the existence of a
general agreement or consensus, or of an overwhelming expert
majority, in favour of some particular theory or policy that is
being advocated. In fact a marked capacity has been revealed
by economists from time to time, for regarding their own
particular views on a question of economic theory or policy as
being generally accepted, by all those qualified to hold an
opinion, as a piece of well-grounded knowledge which only an
ignoramus or even a madman would question.[59]
It would not be doing justice to these claims to treat them
simply as deliberate or conscious exaggerations for polemical or
debating purposes. They seem to be based on genuine illusions
stemming from a deep-seated desire for certainty and authority
and a consequent failure to distinguish between fact and
opinion. Such illusions as to the nature and extent of economic
knowledge and economic ignorance have been remarkably
persistent among economists of all political colours from ultra-
'liberals' to the various brands of 'Marxists'.
In fact, in due course it even came to be held that to have
denied the beneficial effects of devaluation at this time was
epistemologically equivalent to having asserted that the earth was
flat.[60] However, as we have seen, there had been an impressive

list of economist flat-earthers between October 1964 and the end of 1966.[61] Moreover, looking back from 1970 to 1972, further economists apparently proceeded to assert that the earth was flat, or had been from 1964 to 1967.

First, we might cite a detailed statistical study of Britain's Balance of Payments, 1958–1967', by Mr. A. P. Thirlwall, who concluded:

> On the evidence, the Government acted quite responsibly in attempting to control demand before contemplating devaluation. But if the Labour Government was not unwise in rejecting devaluation in 1964, what was the justification in 1967?
>
> The decision to devalue was taken ... against the background of a lack of confidence, not so much in Britain's ability to pay her way through an underlying worsening in her trading position, but in her ability to cope with ... emergencies and contingencies. It was a foreign exchange crisis unrelated to any major crisis on trading account – at least compared with 1964 or 1960... The basic deficit against which Britain devalued ... was considerably less than in 1964.[62]

Secondly, we might cite the summary judgment of Sir Henry Phelps Brown (1972), then President of the Royal Economic Society:

> It appears probable that the parity of sterling maintained from 1949 to 1967 was no major source of difficulty to the balance of payments; and, consequently, that no sharp change of course is to be expected from devaluation...
> Government policy in respect of sterling thus appears not to have exerted a great influence for good or ill.[63]

A *third* retrospective (1972) 'flat-earther', who had opposed devaluation with the same vigour nearly a decade before, was Lord Balogh, who now explained:

The neo-Keynesians ... disappointed in the inefficacy of fiscal and monetary gadgeteering, turned in desperation towards 'flexible' exchanges – creeping, crawling, floating freely (clean) or in a managed way (dirty). All of them had forgotten that devaluation is no easy way out... *The devaluation effect, as a very few of us asserted on earlier experience, was disappointing.* The greater part of the post-devaluation improvement was due to the expansion of world trade and the cost-inflation of the United States... The export surplus and the increasing imbalance of government finance was not able to mitigate the increasingly severe unemployment, which was the factor which held other inflows down... *The miracles neo-Keynesians believed in cannot be expected...*[64]

Lord Balogh maintained that if advice to devalue in the autumn of 1964 had been followed, 'the Labour Government would have come to a sticky end before 1966'.[65] Clearly, for Lord Balogh, exchange-rate policy must have regard to the survival in office of a particular party. Lord Balogh continued by noting that, in 1967, '*when devaluation came it was utterly mismanaged*',[66] and, with an eye to the future, proclaimed: 'the utter necessity of an incomes policy if Labour is to have any hope at all'.

Indeed, by February 1975 it was quite like old times. While authorities like Mr. Samuel Brittan were strongly supporting further devaluation or downward-floating, 'flat-earthism' was thoroughly respectable again, with some of those who had been so enthusiastic for devaluation a decade previously, both among 'Keynesians' and among 'monetarists', maintaining,

our calculations strongly suggest that devaluation is not a feasible method for securing a substantial improvement in the trade deficit...

The exchange rate cannot safely be used because devaluation aggravates the price wage spiral.[67]

K

Again we wish to emphasise that we certainly would not necessarily charge with inconsistency those who favoured devaluation in the sixties and opposed it in the seventies. What may be criticised is simply the dogmatism with which the case for devaluation was, in some cases, proclaimed in the sixties and the fantasies that were propagated regarding economists' opinions.

VI

The preceding survey is reasonably, though of course not absolutely, full and representative regarding economists' pronouncements on devaluation between 1964 and 1969.[68] Counting heads has a limited significance in this context, but between 1964 and November 1967 roughly a half of the university economists whose views have been indicated were in favour, and half against. Among the ten or so non-academic, or journalist economists, there was a large majority against. It may well be that among those who were unable or unwilling to state their views publicly, rather more were in favour than against. But what is undeniable is that opinion was significantly divided; that until 1967 there was a substantial body of opinion on either side, and that nothing like a consensus could be said to have existed. It is clear, also, that wide disagreements continued after November 1967 on the measures necessary to make devaluation successful, in spite of a brief temporary lull in controversy. It seems that disagreement will continue as to what was effected by the devaluation of 1967, how far its results were beneficent, and as to how harmful was the failure to devalue earlier. Of course, that differences and disagreements exist and persist on such issues, including their positive aspects, does not *necessarily* imply that there is something wrong with economics and economists. But it is clear that the contribution of what is called 'exchange-rate theory' to decisions or opinions about devaluation is very limited, and that its predictive potential, though not quite negligible, is tenuous and elusive in view of the considerable range of qualifications or assumptions on which the so-called 'theory' depends.

As regards policy pronouncements, a good deal of disagreement and ambiguity may have stemmed from the failure to specify sufficiently clearly or precisely the *objectives* which were being assumed. Obviously the primary but instrumental objective was to 'improve' the balance of payments. But advocacy of, or opposition to, devaluation, as compared with other means, obviously turned on its effects on such objectives as employment, distribution, and growth.

The wide range of variegated effects which devaluation might have were lumped together into some aggregate, and judged 'favourable' or 'unfavourable to Britain' (as also in the remarkable economists' referendum on British entry into Europe). Linked with this oversimplification of objectives was the fallacy of suggesting, or implying, that 'experts' can decide precisely what is the 'correct' exchange rate (which, in fact, they can be no more competent to pronounce upon than they can be on what is the 'correct' level of employment or the 'correct' rate of inflation).[69]

Given the nature of the material it is not to be expected, nor even desired, that there should not be wide disagreements on such an issue, quite apart from different normative or political value-judgments regarding desirable objectives. But that disagreements, simply on the positive issues, are inevitable, does not justify, but, on the contrary, renders all the more *un*justifiable, the dogmatic overconfidence regarding the correctness of views, on one side or the other, or the comparison of opposing views with beliefs in the flatness of the earth. There is obviously revealed here a considerable misconception about the nature of economic knowledge and ignorance, which comes down from a century and a half previously when James Mill and McCulloch were comparing the leading classical 'laws' (such as those of markets and of natural wages) with the propositions of Newton, and when denying the classical analysis of saving and investment was likened to asserting the flatness of the earth.

It may well have constituted a valid contribution for economists to have urged, in general theoretical terms, that considerable advantages might have been derived from devaluation, *if the operation was timed and executed with sufficient skill.* But such a general theoretical contribution would have lost much, or all, or even more than all, of its value, if it was not sufficiently appreciated how wide is the gap between setting out general theoretical possibilities and successful practical, political applications. As Edgeworth insisted:

> It is only at the heights that contemplation 'reigns and revels'. The descent to particulars is broken and treacherous; requiring caution, patience, attention to each step. Those who without regarding what is immediately before them have looked away to general views have slipped.[70]

Moreover, the argument is not negligible that policies like devaluation and floating rates simply, in the longer, or not so much longer, run, pay out more rope to the politicians.

Corresponding with the misconceived epistemological dogmatism with which the advocacy of devaluation was often pursued, there was frequently revealed a quite excessive overoptimism regarding the ease and simplicity with which a successful devaluation could be carried out and regarding the scarcely qualified beneficence of the effects. In such ways the excessive expectations of politicians and public regarding the fruits of governmental policies, were heightened. It was always the latest fashionable manoeuvre, like the latest party political programme, which was going to do the trick and bring about some kind of British economic miracle.

VII

By way of an appendix to this appendix we might mention briefly a further major issue in these years which gave rise to some remarkable myths regarding economists' opinions. On the subject of the economic effects of entering the European

Economic Community the capacity for fantasy and myth-making, which we have just noticed with regard to economists' views on devaluation, was again in evidence. Moreover, on this issue the fruits may be contemplated of what was almost certainly, in quantitative terms, by far the largest operation ever mounted in Britain in order to bring to bear the superior qualifications of professional economic opinion on a major issue of current policy.

Regarding myths that had been propagated in 1971, Professor Alan Day felt justified in complaining that the claim had

been assiduously put around ... that there is no economist of standing in Britain who now thinks that there is an economic case for joining the Six.[71]

In fact, Mr. P. Oppenheimer had claimed that only

a few economists can be found who choose to believe in an economic case for joining [the EEC].[72]

Again, as on the devaluation issue, Professor Beckerman was subsequently claiming:

There were two issues on which professional economists were *very nearly unanimous*, namely, devaluation and entry into the Common Market... Almost all economists maintained that, on balance, we would lose economically from entry into the Common Market.[73]

Such statements were (or had been) shown to be devoid of any factual foundation thanks to an extraordinary demonstration of professional economic expertise in the columns of *The Times*. This demonstration, or 'referendum', was organised by two leading trend-setters among economists in Britain, Lord Kaldor and Professor H. G. Johnson, who had both ardently campaigned against British entry into the EEC.[74] It seems permissible to mention the possibility that the organisers, in launching this operation, may, conceivably, have been influenced by such fantasy-claims as those cited above regarding the overwhelming preponderance of economists' views being *against* British entry, and were expecting that these claims would be substantiated rather than demolished by a 'referendum'. (In fact, it may well be that it is even more difficult for economists to predict their colleagues' views on controversial issues than it is to predict many or most kinds of economic behaviour.) Anyhow, the organisers laid considerable emphasis on the 'professional' standing, and superior qualifications, of economists. In an 'urgent' letter (of 11 October 1971) circulated to their colleagues, Lord Kaldor and Professor Johnson maintained (italics added):

> It would be *very important* to know, from the point of view of the British public, where the professional economists of Britain stand on this issue. Everybody agrees that the question is a complex one and that *economists are better qualified than other people to make up their minds on the economic issues one way or the other*.

The question on which economists were urged 'to make up their minds' was formulated in the following terms: *whether or not*

> the economic effects of joining the Common Market, taking both short and long-term effects into account, are more likely to be favourable than unfavourable to Britain.

To describe this question as 'complex' seems a considerable understatement. It consists of a multi-dimensional package in which numerous short- and long-range predictions of a most uncertain kind, as well as various kinds of normative value-judgments, were very much mixed up. For example, positive predictions or guesses regarding the effects of joining the

Common Market on the rate of growth, or on the distribution of income, or on the power of trade unions, or on other economic phenomena, were likely to vary widely as between one economist and another. At the same time, the normative valuations, or weightings, of these different estimated effects, including the preferred trade-offs between such effects (as, say, more growth and less trade union power, or *vice versa*), might diverge even more widely. Consequently economists making *quite different positive predictions* might, if they also held *quite different valuations or 'weightings' regarding trade-offs*, be found on the *same* side of the crude dichotomy (and *vice versa*). But for whatever purpose this exercise was designed, it was not for that of bringing to bear any kind of refined, expert analysis for the benefit of readers of *The Times*. Nevertheless, some economists whose outstanding qualifications seemed to have been concentrated in the area of the most rigorously refined and abstract mathematical analysis were happy to contribute to the exercise (e.g. Professor F. H. Hahn).

The final result of the referendum was apparently 222 signatures on the side of the economic effects of joining the EEC being 'favourable', with 196 'unfavourable', and 99 'undecided'.[75] A regional analysis of these figures revealed that the largest majority of those judging the economic effects 'favourable' was to be found in Scotland, while it was in Oxbridge, London, and the universities of the south-east, that the largest majority judged the economic effects to be *un*favourable. Turning to explanations of this disparity *the only hypotheses put forward by Professor Johnson and Mr. Khan were as follows*:

One tentative hypothesis would concern the extent to which *people in remote places take their opinion from newspapers and television broadcasts*, both of which tended fairly strongly to favour entry. Another might be based on the notion of an 'establishment' opinion, centred on London and the older universities and its opposition to entry as a threat to its independence in governing the country.[76]

We are not, of course, concerned here to appraise these two hypotheses, only to note that they were apparently *the only two considered worthy of mention*. Both hypotheses completely contradicted the claims, on which the exercise had been based, about 'professionalism' and about economists being 'better qualified than other people to make up their minds on the economic issues'. According to Professor Johnson and Mr. Khan, if a group of economists judged the economic effects of entry to be favourable the first explanation to be put forward was that they had been more exposed to newspapers and television, alleged to be predominantly in favour of entry. On the other hand, the first explanation coming to mind for a group of economists in Oxbridge and London considering the economic effects to be *un*favourable was that they were protecting their vested interests in influencing British economic policy (which they had so successfully influenced during the previous decades).

As regards the electorate for this referendum, this was defined as 'the full-time teaching officers of Economics in British universities'.

The reason for this limitation was explained by Lord Kaldor and Professor Johnson as being that 'there is no accepted definition of what constitutes "a professional economist"'.[77]

The size of the total electorate on this basis was not revealed, so that the precise response-rate is not clear. But it seems that the 'turn-out' may have been considerably raised by the perhaps reasonable and defensible calculation, that, as one signatory on the 'favourable' side put it, although the whole performance was 'meaningless',

> since he knew that certain 'antis' would not hesitate to sign, he signed the 'pro' letter to stop them getting away with it.[78]

However, in spite of such calculations and pressures, to which it may well have been justifiable to yield, it seems that the number of abstainers, with the addition of the 'undecideds', must have outnumbered, perhaps very considerably, the total of signatories on the two sides. This seems to have been perhaps the only intellectually reassuring feature of the whole performance, which nevertheless remains, in quantitative terms, overwhelmingly the largest exercise ever mounted for bringing to bear what was claimed to be professional expert opinion, with superior qualifications, on a major issue of economic policy.

Notes

Introduction

1. It is not simply a rather pedantic terminological point which is involved here. There is a substantial question of interpretation – relating to the presence or absence of testable, empirical and predictive content – which is usually fudged over. Incidentally, the distinction we are suggesting seems to have behind it the authority of Alfred Marshall. Writing to J. N. Keynes, Marshall insisted: 'You continually use the word *theory* where I should use analysis. This seems to me in itself to cause confusion.' To Foxwell, Marshall wrote that in economics there is '*no theory to speak of*'. Presumably Marshall meant that the extensive range of analysis, or 'theorems', in economics possessed very little testable, empirical or predictive content. (For these quotations from Marshall's letters I am indebted to Professor R. H. Coase's unpublished paper 'Marshall on Method'.)

2. As the Director of the National Institute of Economic and Social Research has said: '*There are few contemporary economists who would not claim that their work and their ideas are intended to contribute in some degree, however indirectly, to the improvement of a firm, an industry, a national economy or the world as a whole.* And if it is said that some do not claim this, *there are very few who explicitly proclaim the uselessness of their work,* with the vigour which G. H. Hardy once attempted to justify pure mathematics.' (G. D. N. Worswick, 'Is Progress in Economic Science Possible?', *Economic Journal*, March 1972, p. 75, italics added.)

3. The words quoted are from an article entitled 'The Winter of

Our Discontent', by Professor F. H. Hahn (*Economica*, 1973, p. 323), in which are defended recent extremely abstract and simplified refinements of the century-old general equilibrium analysis. (See below the essay on ' "Crisis" in the 'Seventies'.) T. S. Kuhn has remarked how 'social scientists' tend, as, he alleges, natural scientists 'almost never do, to defend their choice of a research problem . . . chiefly in terms of the social importance of achieving a solution'. (*The Structure of Scientific Revolutions*, 2nd ed., 1970, p. 164.)

4. See *Economists and Economic Policy, 1946–1966*, 1968, Ch. 4.
5. *Essays in Persuasion*, 1931, p. 373.
6. *The Long View and the Short*, 1958, p. 380.

Chapter Two

1. 'The idea of economics as positive science makes predictability the test of its performance, the prediction of relationships in situations not previously observed, as well as the prediction of future events, which in some ways is the acid test.' (G. D. N. Worswick, *Economic Journal*, March 1972, p. 80.)
2. For example, Professor F. H. Hahn has stated: 'One need only think of the amount of misery which has been averted by the demonstration that the arguments for balanced budgets are false to agree that economics can do good even when it does not predict.' (*On the Notion of Equilibrium in Economics*, 1973, p. 41.) Obviously there is a misconception here. If economists did not, or could not, attempt even the simplest kind of predictions about the effects of fiscal policies because such effects were completely unpredictable, then they could not contribute to policy-making in this field. Any propositions about balanced or unbalanced budgets can only 'do good', or 'avert misery', if *some* capacity to predict exists and is being applied.
3. For a discussion of claims by economists (e.g. Sir Roy Harrod) that economists can give authoritative advice without, or beyond, the power to predict see my *'Positive' Economics and Policy Objectives*, 1964, pp. 89 ff.
4. L. M. Lachmann, in *Metroeconomica*, 1959. Quoted by G. L. S. Shackle, as motto of *Epistemics and Economics*, 1972 (italics added).
5. 'I must say, dogmatically if you like, that prediction or control,

or both, do not and cannot apply in a literal sense to social
science... Science in this sense – knowledge used for prediction
and control – simply does not apply in a society with freedom
and equality.' (F. H. Knight, *Intelligence and Democratic
Action*, 1960, p. 69.)

6. *Journal of Economic History*, September 1964, p. 364. Certainly
a subject may exist as a serious intellectual pursuit without
contributing in terms of 'successful prediction'. But the question
which then has to be pressed is *precisely how*, if it is *so* unsuccessful in terms of prediction, economists can subtantiate the traditional aims and claims of their subject – seldom or never frankly
and explicitly abandoned – in tems of real-world usefulness and
fruitfulness, increasing the wealth of nations, and reducing
poverty and unemployment etc., etc. It might also be demanded
just what it is that such rapidly increasing numbers of economists
are being recruited and paid to do by business and governments,
if they are unable to contribute to improved predictions.

7. As Sir Alec Cairncross has said: 'Very little has been written in
the United Kingdom about economic forecasting... To an
economist it is a little shocking that forecasting should have been
so long neglected as a subject of study.' Sir Alec adds, quite
justifiably in our view: 'Anyone who jests at economic forecasting – as everyone does from time to time – is really expressing his scepticism of the scientific foundations of economics'
(*Essays in Economic Management*, 1971, p. 123). On the other
hand, in German the subject has been by no means neglected
and there is an extensive and serious literature. For a survey of
this see A. Schöpf, *Das Prognoseproblem in der Nationalökonomie*, 1966.

8. For example, at the celebration of the centenary, in 1876, of
The Wealth of Nations, by the London Political Economy Club,
Robert Lowe, the Chancellor of the Exchequer, claimed: 'The
test of science is prevision or prediction, and Adam Smith
appears to me in the main to satisfy that condition. He was able
to foresee what would happen, and to build upon that foresight
the conclusions of his science.' (v. Political Economy Club,
*Revised Report of the Proceedings at the Dinner of 31st May
1876*, 1876, p. 7.)

9. *L'Art de la Conjecture*, n.d. p. 226.

10. *Conjectures and Refutations*, 1963, p. 339.

11. As Professor M. G. Kendall has put it: 'It is not possible to doubt, I think, that patterns of behaviour exist in the social sciences in a quantifiable form. But it may legitimately be doubted whether they can be called laws in the sense used in the physical sciences.' ('Natural Law in the Social Sciences', *Journal of the Royal Statistical Society*, 1961, p. 3.)

12. 'There is a substantive difference between the predictions of sociology and those of *some* natural sciences in which the number of conditional influences can be limited by experimental insulation. It also means that there is some substantive difference between sociological predictions and those of any natural science because of the far greater difficulty of assessing the relative importance of various factors in social causation. It does not mean that social phenomena are quite unpredictable; predictability does not imply determinism.' (P. Cohen, in *Problems in the Philosophy of Science*, ed. I. Lakatos and A. Musgrave, 1968, p. 419.)

13. *Economic Forecasts and Policy*, 2nd ed., 1961, pp. 11–14.

14. *Economic Journal*, March 1964, p. 194 (italics added).

15. Op. cit., 1st ed., 1963 and 3rd ed., 1971, pp. 13–14.

16. *The Poverty of Historicism*, 2nd ed., 1960, p. 115.

17. Op. cit., pp. 120–1.

18. *An Introduction to Positive Economics*, 3rd ed., 1971, p. 192. Professor Lipsey was quite justified in criticising the view, which he attributed to Lord Robbins, that economics could not make useful predictions about the real world without *some* knowledge of the stability or instability of particular relations (e.g. that between price and quantity demanded). But Lord Robbins was quite justified in so far as he was simply insisting that figures of elasticities over a period of time could not amount to 'a constant law'. (*Nature and Significance of Economic Science*, 1932, pp. 98–101.)

19. Professor Samuelson has emphasised how unreliable are so-called economic 'laws' which are, in fact, temporary constancies or trends. After describing the consumption function as stating a trend (which Keynes had originally called a 'fundamental psychological law, upon which we are entitled to depend, with great confidence') Professor Samuelson goes on to claim that he has 'learned how treacherous are economic "laws" in economic life: e.g. Bowley's Law of constant relative wage share; Long's

Law of constant population participation in the labour force;
Pareto's Law of unchangeable inequality of incomes; Denison's
Law of constant private saving ratio; Colin Clark's Law of a
25 per cent ceiling on government expenditure and taxation;
Modigliani's Law of constant wealth–income ratio; Marx's Law
of the falling rate of real wage and/or the falling rate of profit;
Everybody's Law of a constant capital–output ratio. If these be
Laws Mother Nature is a criminal by nature.' (v. *Keynes's
General Theory, Reports of Three Decades*, ed. R. Lekachman,
1964, p. 336.) It is certainly justifiable to deny Law-like status to
these so-called 'Laws'. Nevertheless, these fleeting or temporary
trends and tendencies are what economists have to try to spot or
capture as essential material on which to attempt to build less
inaccurate predictions.

20. On the other hand, it would be dangerously misleading to foster
the notion that 'Mother Nature' ultimately prohibits *nothing*
(except, of course, logical or mathematical contradictions) and
that anything and everything is possible, however Utopian, for
policy-makers and 'social engineers'. In a way, it may have
been pardonable for the classical economists to try to keep
politicians and public overawed by their great ineluctable
'Laws'. But the pretence was duly shown up that these Laws
were either vacuous or inaccurately formulated, and this
exposure encouraged Utopian delusions regarding human and
social possibilities. The point is not that 'Mother Nature' may
not impose 'laws' in the social and economic cosmos, but that
such 'laws', if they exist, must be extremely complex and
perhaps changing; and that in any case, *we do not know, at all
precisely, at any particular moment – and may well never
know – just what they are, or have been.*

21. v. Bertrand de Jouvenel, *L'Art de la Conjecture*, n.d., pp. 24
and 91.

22. 'Is Progress in Economic Science Possible?', *Economic Journal*,
March 1972, p. 85. Only three years later Mr. Worswick seemed
to become rather less optimistic: 'It may well be that there are
limits to the extent to which forecasting can be improved: it
could even be that macro-economic forecasting is not far from
those limits. . . It is important that policy-makers and public
should not be deluded as to the possibility of improved accuracy.'
(See *Modelling the Economy*, ed. G. A. Renton, 1975, p. 74.)

23. T. C. Koopmans, *Three Essays on the State of Economic Science*, 1957, p. 212, quoted by A. Lowe, *On Economic Knowledge*, 1965, p. 5.

24. *Forecasting the United Kingdom Economy*, J. C. K. Ash and D. J. Smyth, 1973, p. 263.

25. *Essays in Economic Management*, by Sir Alec Cairncross, 1971, p. 138. It has recently been stated regarding the years 1954–74: 'The record of demand management during the last twenty years has been extremely poor', due significantly to the inadequacies of 'conventional forecasting systems'. One can only ask 'poor' *in relation to what*? Surely not in relation to the previous twenty years. Presumably in relation to what is being *promised*, regarding which it may be prudent to wait and see (v. Memorandum by F. Cripps, W. Godley and M. Fetherston, *Ninth Report from the Expenditure Committee*, 1974, p. 1).

26. J. C. K. Ash and D. J. Smyth, *Forecasting the United Kingdom Economy*, 1973, pp. 54 and 251. Ash and Smyth actually conclude that 'the relative forecasting performance of the Treasury has declined' because it is estimated that 'the economy was easier to forecast in the 1963–1971 period than in the 1951–1962 period' (p. 54). But their conclusion that the economy became easier to predict does not seem necessarily to follow, as they claim it does, from the improved performance of 'naive' models which simply extrapolate past changes (v. M. J. C. Surrey, *Economic Journal*, December 1974, pp. 1012–13). It is *very* difficult to assess predictive accuracy when predictions do not, or cannot feasibly, take account of policy changes or other reactions which may often be prompted by the announcement of the predictions. The same reservation seems to apply to the nevertheless somewhat sobering conclusion that 'the OECD half-yearly forecasts are no better than those generated by naive forecasts, ... and that the accuracy of OECD forecasts, relative to naive predictions, shows no significant improvement over time' (D. J. Smyth and J. C. K. Ash, *Economic Journal*, June 1975, p. 364). A survey of its own forecasts by the National Institute of Economic and Social Research of its record from 1959 to 1967 concluded that there has been 'no striking changes in forecasting accuracy between the two periods' (*N.I.E. Review*, November 1969, p. 46).

27. 'This massive injection of speed and novelty into the fabric of

society will force us not merely to cope more rapidly with
familiar situations, events and moral dilemmas, but to cope at a
progressively faster rate with situations that are, for us, decidedly
unfamiliar, "first-time" situations, strange, irregular, unpredictable. This will significantly alter the balance that prevails
in any society between the familiar and unfamiliar elements in
the daily life of its people, between the routine and non-routine,
the predictable and unpredictable.' (A. Toffler, *Future Shock*,
p. 201.)

28. *Principles of Political Economy*, ed. W. J. Ashley, 1909, p. 242.
29. *Papers Relating to Political Economy*, vol. I, 1925, p. 138.
    Edgeworth writes: 'This theoretical difference between the
    regime of monopoly and that of competition may have some
    bearing on practical issues, affecting as it does our views about
    trade unions and similar combinations. I have seen it proposed
    as an economic ideal that every branch of trade and industry
    should be formed into a separate union. The picture has some
    attractions. Nor is it at first sight morally repulsive; since, where
    all are monopolists, no one will be the victim of monopoly. But
    an attentive consideration will disclose an incident very
    prejudicial to industry – instability in the value of all those
    articles the demand for which is influenced by the prices of
    other articles; a class which is probably very extensive.' (Perhaps
    it would have been more apposite for Edgeworth, instead of
    '*instability*', to have written 'unpredictability'.)
30. See the illuminating discussion by Professor K. W. Rothschild
    who emphasises that the inadequate treatment of non-, or extra-
    economic factors often amounts to 'a fatal weakness', which
    'turns many economic predictions simply into conditional
    predictions of dubious applicability' (*Wirtschaftsprognose,
    Methoden und Probleme*, 1969, pp. 18–19). Stanislav Andreski
    makes a similar point in his brilliant volume *Social Sciences as
    Sorcery* (1972, p. 140): 'The evolution towards diffuse pluralistic
    collectivism, involving growing interpenetration of government,
    pressure groups and the organs of economic control, has con-
    siderably enlarged the discrepancy between current reality and
    the tacit sociological assumptions of economic theory (which
    applies even to such recent additions to it as the Keynesian
    models): but the arbitrary nature of these assumptions has been
    fully revealed only when the conclusions about the affairs of

under-developed countries, drawn on the basis of conventional economic theory, have proved to be manifestly false.'
31. Alan Day, *The Observer*, 28 November 1971.

Chapter Three
1. As the author, long ago, of one of these slim volumes, I would not want to suggest that abstract, largely normative essays are necessarily useless, or worse. But returns to general abstract methodological arguments are apt to diminish rather sharply for those whose interests are primarily centred on their own particular subject. Regarding the views expressed in that earlier essay (*The Significance and Basic Postulates of Economic Theory, 1938 and 1960*), I would still support for economics the criteria of testability and falsifiability. However, though this early essay could be claimed to have been, in many ways, a sceptical work by the standards of 1938, its optimistic 'naturalism' seems now indefensible: that is, its suggestions that the 'social sciences' could and would develop in the same manner as physics and the natural sciences. This is certainly not now to assert that economists and 'social scientists' *should not try* to follow natural scientific methods, and the 'mature' sciences, *as far as they can, while respecting the nature of their material*. In fact economists have achieved *some* degree of success along these lines. But it should not be imagined or suggested that they can 'succeed' – and, above all, not be pretended that they have 'succeeded' – in anything approaching the same manner as has been achieved in physics and other natural sciences. Whether these differences between economics and physics are regarded as a matter of degree or a matter of principle does not seem to be very important as long as their full significance is understood. However, it seems highly misleading to insist on certain general similarities between the natural and social sciences (although such general similarities certainly exist), and to assert that the differences are only ones 'of degree', *without* making it clear how important in practice these differences are.
2. For example, regarding 'disagreement about facts' Oskar Lange wrote: '*Such disagreement can always be removed by further observation* and study of the empirical material. Frequently,

L

however, the empirical data necessary to resolve the disagreement are unavailable. In such cases the issue remains unsettled.
The conclusion that the issue cannot be settled with the data
available has interpersonal validity. *Agreement is reached to
withhold judgment*' ('The Scope and Method of Economic
Science', from *Review of Economic Studies*, No. 13, 1945–6
reprinted in *Readings in the Philosophy of Science*, ed. H. Feigl
and M. Brodbeck, 1953, p. 748, italics added). The notion of
real-world economists, on any considerable scale, actually
reaching agreement to 'withhold judgment', because adequate
empirical data to resolve disagreements are unavailable, is,
unfortunately, as fantastic as is a model of real-world firms and
households generally returning smoothly and rapidly to some
ideal equilibrium position.

3. Cf. Paul Feyerabend: 'Whenever I read Kuhn, I am troubled
by the following question: are we here presented with
methodological prescriptions which tell the scientist how to
proceed: or are we given a description, void of any evaluative
element, of those activities which are generally called
"scientific"?' Kuhn's answer does not seem entirely satisfactory
when he maintains that he is concerned with both description
and prescription, *at once*, because 'scientists should behave
essentially as they do if their concern is to improve scientific
knowledge'. Whatever may be claimed on behalf of physicists,
it seems doubtful whether *economists* have always behaved
exactly as they would if their sole concern is, or had been, to
'improve economic knowledge'. On the other hand, criticising
Lakatos, Kuhn writes: 'What Lakatos conceives as history is not
history at all, but philosophy fabricating examples.' (See
Criticism and the Growth of Knowledge, ed. I. Lakatos and
A. Musgrave, 1970, pp. 198 and 237; and 'History of Science
and its Rational Reconstruction', *Boston Studies in the
Philosophy of Science*, VIII, 1971, p. 143).

4. The history of recent or contemporary policy proposals and
doctrines seems particularly significant in economics as revealing
the kind of claims regarding effective economic knowledge
entertained by economists. However, this is not to be recommended as an area in which a forthright account of the fruits of
his research will be likely to promote the professional popularity
of the researcher (see Appendix).

5. *Encyclopaedia of the Social Sciences*, vol. XIV, 1968, p. 76.
6. *Scientific Knowledge and its Social Problems*, 1971, pp. 173 and 410.
7. Irving Kristol, *The Observer*, 4 October 1964.
8. A somewhat similar suggestion in terms of the mildly historicist concept of 'underdevelopment' (rather than 'immaturity') has been made by Sir Henry Phelps Brown, as the conclusion of his Presidential address to the Royal Economic Society entitled, 'The Underdevelopment of Economics'. Professor Phelps Brown concludes that economics 'has hardly yet reached its 17th century. I believe we shall make better progress when we realise how far we still have to go' (*Economic Journal* March 1972, p. 10). It is not that one should question the healthy and realistic message that economics is in a very different epistemological position from that of physics. What should be questioned is the implication that economics is progressing along the same kind of road as physics, towards the same kind of goal or destination, to be reached in due course, though at the moment two or three hundred years away. Professor Phelps Brown cites in support Professor Morgenstern's conclusion that 'the principal condition for the advancement of economics is still to improve the empirical background. . . Our knowledge of the relevant facts of economics is incomparably smaller than that commanded in physics when the mathematisation of the subject was achieved . . . backed by several millennia of systematic scientific, astronomical observation. . . Nothing of this sort has occurred in economic science.' But it should be emphasised, by way of a significant major addition to this argument, that the millennia of systematic astronomical observation were concerned with *mainly constant or stable phenomena*, in contrast with most economic observation. This point strengthens still further Professor Phelps Brown's condemnation of the neglect of history by economists. (v. O. Morgenstern, 'Limits to the Uses of Mathematics in Economics', in *Mathematics and Social Sciences Monograph*, June 1965, pp. 12-29; and *The Theory of Games and Economic Behaviour*, 3rd ed., 1955, para. 1.2.4). On Professor Phelps Brown's criticisms, see below on 'Crisis in the Seventies, the Crisis of Abstraction'.
9. *Nicomachaean Ethics*, translated by W. D. Ross, 1915, ch. 3

L*

(quoted by J. R. Ravetz, *Scientific Knowledge and its Social Problems*, 1971, p. 158n.).

10. See the article by Professor M. J. Roberts, 'On the Nature and Condition of Social Science', in *Daedalus*, Summer 1974: 'Social science has accomplished less than it might because social scientists have inappropriately tried to imitate certain character-istics of natural science, especially physics. Social scientists have not understood that the nature of the particular phenomena they study has implications both for how they should proceed and what they can hope to find out. . . This view implies giving up the notion that there is some close analogy in the social sciences to basic research in the physical sciences. With complex heterogeneous objects that have many characteristics, we can hope to discern only limited regularities. . . This makes the typical task of social science less glamorous, less general, and more expensive than it has generally been considered.' (Op. cit., pp. 47 and 62.)

11. *The Philosophy of Karl Popper*, ed. Schlipp, 1974, p. 96.

12. *The Open Society and its Enemies*, revised ed. 1962, vol. I, p. 2, and vol. II, p. 9.

13. *The Poverty of Historicism*, 2nd ed., 1960, pp. 1 and 16.

14. *Criticism and the Growth of Knowledge*, ed. I. Lakatos and A. Musgrave, 1970, p. 57; and *The Philosophy of Karl Popper*, ed. Schlipp, 1974, p. 14.

15. Op. cit., p. 60n.

16. *The Poverty of Historicism*, 2nd ed., 1960, pp. 61–2. I have commented before on this argument of Popper's regarding economic 'laws', when discussing prediction in economics: see *'Positive' Economics and Policy Objectives*, 1964, p. 95.

17. J. G. Kemeny, *A Philosopher Looks at Science*, 1959, p. 244. The following conclusion of Barrington Moore may also be noted: 'Social science, after some two hundred years, has not yet discovered any universal propositions comparable in scope or intellectual significance to those in the natural sciences. . . Classical economics managed to erect at one time a compre-hensive and elegant theory to organise its subject matter in a scientific manner. Somehow the facts have changed since the formulation of the theory. . . We do not yet have any laws in social science comparable to those in the natural sciences.' (*Political Power and Social Theory*, 1958, pp. 127–8.) However,

economists, both orthodox and Marxist, from Ricardo to Robbins, *until quite recently*, have had no compunction about proclaiming Economic Laws (often with capital letters) in a most impressive manner. This insistence upon strict laws in the economic cosmos may have had healthy intentions, and briefly some healthy effects in countering the Utopian delusions of politicians and public. But it was bound to be found out and to lead to even more wildly Utopian reactions.

18. Op. cit., p. 143 (italics added).
19. 'On the Nature and Condition of Social Science', *Daedalus*, Summer 1974, p. 58.
20. *Criticism and the Growth of Knowledge*, ed. I. Lakatos and A. Musgrave, 1970, pp. 244–5.
21. See the previous chapter on 'Prediction and Economic Knowledge'.
22. Op. cit., p. 247.
23. *Scientific Knowledge and its Social Problems*, 1971, p. 366.
24. Op. cit., p. 396. A similar conclusion is propounded by Professor S. Andreski in his trenchant essay '*Social Sciences as Sorcery*' (Pelican ed., 1974, pp. 149–51): 'The sophisticated mathematical models, which one finds in books on economics, might mislead an unwary reader into believing that he is facing something equivalent to the theories of physics. . . It is important to bear in mind that even in the branch which has opportunities for measurement unrivalled in the other social sciences, an infatuation with numbers and formulae can lead to empirical irrelevance and fraudulent postures of expertise. The most pernicious manifestations of the last-named tendency (abetted by the natural proclivity of every occupation to extol its wares) have been the claims of numerous economists to act as arbiters on matters of planning, on the assumption (whose efficacy depends on its being tacitly made rather than explicitly recognised) that the factors which can be measured must serve as the basis for decision. . . The assumption in question has often led economists to aid and abet the depredations of a soul-destroying and world-polluting commercialism, by silencing the defenders of aesthetic and humane values with the trumpets of one-sided statistics.'
25. Op. cit., p. 369.
26. Op. cit., p. 159.

27. Op. cit., p. 378. Professor Marc J. Roberts has made a similar point: 'The failure of economists to make clear how little they know or can hope to know is understandable. Society seems to be most generous to and respectful of the "real sciences". Material well-being, power, status, and the scientist's ability to "fulfil his moral obligations" by influencing policy – all these depend on the acceptance by the wider society of his expertise. And when politics become involved, the chances increase that more will be promised than can be delivered, especially by the political actors in whose retinue social scientists are enlisted. . . The pressures on contemporary social scientific guilds have prevented a full and frank assessment of this situation. Accomplishments have often been oversold.' ('On the Nature and Condition of Social Science', *Daedalus*, Summer 1974, pp. 58 and 61.)

28. Op. cit., p. 400. The following is from a review of a leading textbook of econometrics: 'Anyone reading this book could be excused if he were left with the impression that at last Economics has become a Science. For here are set out first the underlying mathematical techniques, then the mathematical structure of the various econometric models, the techniques of estimation of the parameter values and the properties of the estimators obtainable. Problems are duly provided at appropriate points in the text, and there are half a dozen or more tables of down-to-earth statistics which form the basis of many further tables illustrating techniques of estimation. *One almost has to pinch oneself to keep in mind that it is highly dubious whether the structure of the determination of the variables in the real world approximates the structure of the theoretical models for which this impressive apparatus of thought is designed to provide parameter estimates.* However, it would be as churlish to blame an author expounding econometrics for the fact that the real world can seldom be fruitfully studied by econometric methods, as it would be to criticise a monarch for taking part in pageantry which has no immediate practical utility.' (Professor D. G. Champernowne, *Economic Journal*, 1972, pp. 222–3, italics added.) The comment might be added that it seems that it would probably be *much more* 'churlish' to blame the monarch than the econometrician. Anyhow, the comparison is quite far-reaching: decisions have to get taken in a world of ignorance and uncertainty. It may be

desirable socially that there should be a certain confidence in the
decisions and the decision-makers, however profound and
inevitable their ignorance. The magic of monarchy and
traditional deference having faded as sources of reassurance, the
'professional' mysteries of mathematical model-building and
'*expertise*' take their place. (I am indebted for the quotation to
Professor D. P. O'Brien's distinguished inaugural lecture,
Whither Economics?, Durham, 1974, p. 19.)

29. Op. cit., p. 401.
30. *Criticism and the Growth of Knowledge*, ed. I. Lakatos and
    A. Musgrave, 1970, p. 93, and 'History of Science and its
    Rational Reconstruction', in *Boston Studies in the Philosophy of
    Science*, VIII, ed. R. S. Cohen and C. R. Buck, 1971, pp. 122
    and 133.
31. Lakatos and Musgrave, op. cit., p. 179n. Two years earlier
    Lakatos had insisted *in much stronger terms* that 'the reluctance
    of economists . . . *was primarily*' (not '*may have been partly*')
    due etc. (v. *Proceedings of the Aristotelian Society*, 1968, p. 183).
32. Lakatos and Musgrave, op. cit., p. 151.
33. 'Situational Determinism in Economics', in *The British Journal
    for the Philosophy of Science*, 1972, p. 237. Actually, Professor
    Machlup's criticism, discussed by Dr. Latsis, is criticism of this
    writer. It might be assumed that Professor Lakatos himself did
    not disagree with Dr. Latsis's description.
34. 'Research Programmes in Economics', *Nafplion*, 1974, p. 18.
35. Op. cit., p. 19.
36. Op. cit., pp. 20, 21, 22 and 25 (italics added).
37. Op. cit., p. 16.
38. 'History of Science and its Rational Reconstruction', *Boston
    Studies in the Philosophy of Science*, VIII, ed. R. S. Cohen and
    C. R. Buck, 1971, pp. 121 and 133.
39. See *Economists and Economic Policy 1946–1966*, 1968, pp. 213–
    216.
40. *Criticism and the Growth of Knowledge*, ed. I. Lakatos and
    A. Musgrave, 1970, p. 229. Professor Alan Musgrave has
    expressed, in an unpublished paper, his agreement with Professor
    Feyerabend 'that "anything goes" is the position which Lakatos
    has finally adopted. . . As it stands, therefore, his methodology
    gives *carte blanche* to any group who wants to erect their pet
    notion into a dogma.' Professor Musgrave emphasises some close

parallels and similarities between the methodological criteria of
Kuhn and Lakatos. (See 'Falsification and its Critics', in *Logic,
Methodology and Philosophy of Science*, ed. P. Suppes *et al.*,
1973, p. 400, and Professor Musgrave's unpublished revision of
this paper which I am most grateful for having been shown.)

41. *Criticism and the Growth of Knowledge*, ed. I. Lakatos and
A. Musgrave, 1970, p. 93 (italics added). As an example of this
kind of exploitation of Kuhn's views (unintended by Kuhn
himself) by a well-known 'radical' economist, we might cite the
statement of Dr. Rose Dugdale: 'Kuhn has cast serious doubts
upon this paragon of the virtues of objectivity – the natural
sciences. After all it is not at all clear that science advances as
Popper would have us believe, from hypothesis to falsifying
evidence and so the replacement of the hypothesis by a better
theory.' (In *Counter Course*, ed. T. Pateman, 1972, 'Economic
Theory in Class Society', p. 166.)

42. Regarding the 'falsification' principle, Professor Musgrave
emphasises its anti-dogmatic significance: 'To regard a theory as
falsified is, in other words, to be aware of a problem: . . . Should
falsified theories be rejected? Well, if "rejected" means
"rejected as being false" then the answer is obviously "Yes".
But if rejected means "rejected as not being the best available
theory" then the answer is equally obviously "No, not necessarily".' Professor Musgrave also objects to 'the needless para-
doxes . . . created by arguing that since theories which have been
empirically falsified are not "rejected" or "eliminated" or
"scrapped", they cannot really have been falsified at all'. In fact,
'it is the peculiarities of the scientific context which will in large
part determine how an apparent refutation will be handled'.
(See 'Falsification and its Critics', in *Logic, Methodology and
Philosophy of Science*, ed. P. Suppes *et al.*, 1973, p. 403.)

43. For example in the discussion of 'scientific prediction' in
R. G. Lipsey's *An Introduction to Positive Economics*, 1963–71,
pp. 13–14.

44. As Professor H. G. Johnson has put it (*Encounter*, June 1972,
p. 91): 'In a competition between scholars and political propagandists, the scholar is likely to lose', or, in other words, 'nice
guys finish last'. The 'scholar' may be taken to be someone who
accepts some kind of intellectual discipline rather than 'anything
goes'; and where he is a 'loser' or 'finishes last' *is not in respect*

of the objectives of his discipline, scholarship, or 'science', but in terms of political influence and power – which is what some economic 'experts' are primarily or *exclusively* after. They therefore tend to follow the principles (without perhaps professing them so openly) of that robust party-politician, the late Sir Gerald Nabarro MP: 'I am a propagandist. When one is propagating views and ideals, one does not determine too closely what is fact and what is supposition. They are all mixed up together.' However, Sir Gerald did not claim any 'professional' scholarly or 'scientific' status. Nor, either, did he try to invoke the rather feeble, pseudo-philosophical, excuse, much indulged in by 'Marxists' in recent years, that since it is impossible or very difficult or restrictive to keep absolutely, perfectly separate all the time, 'what is fact' from 'what is supposition', therefore there is no obligation to attempt to do so, and so any kind of crude 'Marxist' political propaganda is legitimised.

45. *Memorials of A. Marshall*, ed. A. C. Pigou, 1925, p. 306.

46. *American Economic Review*, September 1964, p. 736. It may now be largely forgotten how long, powerful, and confident the *a priorist* tradition in economics was, coming down from Senior and Cairnes to Wieser and Mises, and maintaining that far from facing greater difficulties, *the economist started* with *great advantages compared with the natural scientist*: 'The economist starts with a knowledge of ultimate causes. He is already, at the outset of his enterprise, in the position which the physicist only attains after ages of laborious research.' (Cairnes.) Moreover: 'We can observe natural phenomena only from outside, but ourselves from within... What a huge advantage for the natural scientist if the organic and inorganic world clearly informed him of its laws, and why should we neglect such assistance?' (Wieser.) No wonder economists have been confident in their policy pronouncements. (v. *The Significance and Basic Postulates of Economic Theory*, 1938, pp. 131ff.) It would have been much more to the point if Professor Samuelson had cited Wieser among the *a priorists* rather than Menger.

47. 'The most characteristic element in this situation seemed to me the incessant stream of confirmations, of observations which "verified" the theories in question, and this point was constantly emphasized by their adherents. A Marxist could not open a newspaper without finding on every page confirming evidence

for his interpretation of history; not only in the news, but also in
its presentation – which revealed the class bias of the paper – and
especially of course in what the papers did *not* say.' (*Conjectures
and Refutations*, 1963, p. 35.) See, on the other hand, Popper's
denial that his interpretation of the methods of science was
'influenced by any knowledge of the methods of the social
sciences' (*The Poverty of Historicism*, 2nd ed., 1960, p. 137).

48. Lord Roberthall, *Economic Journal*, December 1959, p. 651.

49. It may be noted that Professor Milton Friedman is duly cautious
about causation: 'I myself try to avoid the use of the word
"cause", . . . it is a tricky and unsatisfactory word' (*Inflation:
Causes, Consequences, Cures*, I.E.A., 1974, p. 101). But a few
pages away Professor Laidler is insisting: 'What we do argue is
that *the cause* of inflation really is very simple: it is monetary
expansion' (p. 64).

50. 'Keynesian Monetary Theory and the Cambridge School',
Banca Nazionale del Lavoro Quarterly Review, June 1972,
p. 142. But at least Yale and Chicago recognise the desirability
or obligation of trying to produce *some* kind of empirical
evidence. This is, at any rate, in advance of other 'schools'
which have dogmatised for decades, in 'high priori' terms,
about the effects or non-effects of fiscal and monetary policy
without ever having produced any empirical evidence –
verificatory or falsificatory – other than the most casual.

51. 'Our often unconscious views on the theory of knowledge and
its central problems ("What can we know?" "How certain is
our knowledge?"), are decisive for our attitude towards ourselves and towards politics' (*The Philosophy of Karl Popper*,
ed. Schilpp, 1974, p. 91).

52. Nobody has attacked more eloquently and discerningly than
Professor Paul Feyerabend on the *one* hand the dangerous
pretensions of contemporary science, and on the *other* hand the
appalling intellectual pollution of our times. His attacks have a
great deal of significance and even *a fortiori* strong relevance,
regarding 'social science'. Feyerabend complains of science
having 'become too powerful, too pushy, and too dangerous to
be left on its own'. Meanwhile 'illiterate and incompetent books
flood the market, empty verbiage full of strange and esoteric
terms claim to express profound insights, "experts" without
brains, without character, and without even a modicum of

intellectual, stylistic emotional temperament tell us about our
"condition" and the means of improving it' (*Against Method*,
1975, pp. 216–17). It seems all the more strange and perverse
that Professor Feyerabend should be trying to remove and
destroy such critical weapons as are available against *both* of
these dangerous and appalling phenomena (i.e. the weapons of
'falsificationism').

Chapter Four

1. Professor J. K. Galbraith has proclaimed in *The Times* (16 July
   1975): 'On the largest and most important question facing the
   governments of the industrial countries the economic profession
   – I choose my words with care – is intellectually bankrupt. It
   might as well not exist.' This is because economists have not
   succeeded in devising an effective method of incomes control
   and have not devoted as much effort towards this end as they
   might have done. But one can only be 'bankrupt' if one has
   assumed excessive obligations. Some economists certainly have
   not assumed any such obligations and would have been justified
   in regarding their assumption as irresponsible. On the other
   hand, some economists have encouraged over-optimism regarding great 'purposive' programmes of planning for growth, with
   'full employment', which may have required 'incomes controls',
   which these economists have demanded, without effectively
   constructing: they may then have gone on to denounce trade
   union leaders as 'stupid'. This *does* sound rather like 'bank-
   ruptcy'.

2. In the middle decades of the nineteenth century an extraordinary
   degree of confidence in the Science of Political Economy had
   been encouraged and expressed by such influential spokesmen
   for orthodoxy as the two Mills and McCulloch (the latter an
   important pioneer in the history of economic thought).
   McCulloch claimed, for example, that 'the errors with which
   Political Economy was formerly infected have now nearly
   disappeared, and a very few observations will suffice to show
   that it really admits of as much certainty in its conclusions as any
   science founded on fact and experiment can possibly do. . . The
   relation between rent and profit, between profit and wages, and
   the various general laws which regulate and connect the

apparently clashing, but really harmonious interests of every different order in society, have been discovered, and established with all the certainty of demonstrative evidence.' (*A Discourse on the Rise, Progress, Peculiar Objects, and Importance of Political Economy*, 1824, pp. 75 and 81.) McCulloch reprinted this *Discourse*, almost completely unchanged nearly forty years later. James Mill maintained that there was perfect agreement *among all those qualified to hold an opinion (i.e. who agreed with James Mill)*: see Mill's superb essay 'Whether Political Economy is Useful', in *Selected Economic Writings*, ed. D. Winch, 1966). J. S. Mill, though modest on his own behalf, 'was not at all modest on behalf of his time' (as Schumpeter has observed), and added his immense authority and prestige to proclaiming this kind of extremely confident view of the subject (v. *History of Economic Analysis*, 1954, p. 530). Even Senior, who was much more cautious, in explaining to a Frenchman the prosperity and economic leadership of mid-Victorian Britain, claimed the success for the science of political economy: 'It is the triumph of theory. We are governed by philosophers and political economists.' (*Conversations with M. Thiers, M. Guizot, and other Distinguished Persons during the Second Empire*, 1878, vol. I, p. 169, quoted by A. Gerschenkron, *Papers and Proceedings of the American Economic Association*, May 1969, p. 6.)

3. Professor A. G. Hines, *The Times Higher Educational Supplement*, 30 March 1973.

4. V. C. Walsh, *Introduction to Contemporary Microeconomics*, McGraw-Hill, 1970, pp. 3–5. It may be noted that what the 'revolutionaries' were preoccupied with were 'issues *of form*'.

5. It has been estimated that between 1964 and 1975 the growth in numbers of the Government Economic Service was at a compounded annual rate of 28 per cent (v. *The Times*, 24 November 1975, p. 1).

6. Sir Donald MacDougall, *Economic Journal*, December 1974, p. 774. According to *The Economist* (15 June 1974): 'Economists multiply exponentially. In 1962, some 8,000 sixth formers passed "A" level economics compared with, for example, 24,000 who passed in physics. By 1972 economics and physics were running neck and neck at 28,000, with history left behind at 27,000... More economists are actually being employed as economists. Membership of the Society of Business Economists has increased

three-fold in the past decade; the Government economic service
has risen from 16 economists to over 300; even the Bank of
England's little lot have grown from 12 to 45.'

7. Op. cit., p. 774.

8. Business Schools and Management Education were also boom-
ing. *The National Plan*, of 1965 (p. 53), 'expected that over the
next few years the increased quantity and quality of management education of all kinds will be making an important
contribution' (that is, to raising the growth-rate of the British
economy in accordance with the Plan).

9. Another wave of the Great Economic Expansion in Britain took
the form of an extensive development of in-service courses in
economics for civil servants at the Centre for Administrative
Studies. It is not clear what brand of economics was inculcated
at such courses. But Mr. R. Opie (1968) enthusiastically described
the Centre, and its courses in economics, as 'easily the most
important single source of hope for the future'. However, elsewhere in the same volume Professor D. Seers maintained that:
'Particularly dangerous, unless accompanied by deeper structural
reforms, are the in-service training programmes which provide
a smattering of economics and managerial techniques. . . A little
economics is a very dangerous thing.' (So, also, *can be* a lot of
economics, unless, of course, it's of one's own exclusive brand.)
See *Crisis in the Civil Service*, ed. H. Thomas, 1968, pp. 79 and
105.

10. In an attempt subsequently to counter the scepticism encouraged
by their predecessors, two strenuous Presidential attempts at
cheerfulness were undertaken by Sir Donald MacDougall in his
Presidential address to the Royal Economic Society ('In Praise
of Economics', *Economic Journal*, December 1974, pp. 773 ff.),
and by Professor W. Heller ('What's Right with Economics',
Papers and Proceedings of the American Economic Association,
1975). Though to some extent they provide a justifiable counter-
balance, these two attempts at official optimism hardly dealt
with the quite specific fundamental criticisms raised by their
predecessors Professors Phelps Brown and Leontief.

11. *Economic Journal*, March 1972, p. 75 (italics added).

12. *Economic Journal*, March 1972, p. 3 (italics added).

13. Op. cit., pp. 78 and 83 (italics added).

14. *American Economic Review*, 1971, pp. 1–3.

15. *Induction, Growth and Trade, Essays in Honour of Sir Roy Harrod*, ed. W. A. Eltis, M. F. Scott and J. N. Wolfe, 1970, p. 163.

16. *Economic Journal*, March 1972, p. 79.

17. See *Man and the Social Sciences*, ed. W. A. Robson, 1972, p. 20 (italics added).

18. Op. cit., p. 77.

19. Op. cit., p. 162 (italics added). Sir John Hicks has characterised a growth equilibrium model as follows: 'With every step that we have taken to define this Equilibrium model more strictly, the closer has become its resemblance to the old static (or even stationary) Equilibrium model; its bearing upon reality must have come to seem even more remote. It has been fertile in the generation of class-room exercises; but so far as we can yet see, they are exercises, not real problems. *They are not even hypothetical real problems, of the type "what would happen if?" where the "if" is something that could conceivably happen. They are shadows of real problems*, dressed up in such a way that by pure logic we can find solutions for them.' (*Capital and Growth*, 1965, p. 183, italics added.)

20. This is a striking and most distinguished example of what seems in economics to be quite a frequent intellectual or methodological life-cyclical pattern: that is of an eagerly optimistic youthful enthusiasm for extreme abstractions followed at a more mature stage (on the part of those who do eventually mature) by a realistic scepticism, which may even swing too far the other way.

21. Lord Kaldor set out these conditions as including a closed economy, 'perfect knowledge', 'perfect competition', etc.

22. See *Essays on Value and Distribution*, 1960, p. 13 (italics added). In his Introduction Lord Kaldor explains that these earlier arguments 'show an insufficient awareness of the fact that meaningful generalisations about the real world can only be reached as a result of empirical hypotheses, and not by *a priori* reasoning' (p. 3). It is, of course, rather important to possess a 'sufficient awareness' of this fundamental (though not here very precisely expressed) principle: if not, serious misconceptions about economic 'theory' – and seriously over-optimistic misapplications in terms of policy – occur.

23. 'The Irrelevance of Equilibrium Economics', *Economic Journal*, 1972, pp. 1238–9.

24. See *Capital and Growth*, ed. G. C. Harcourt and N. F. Laing, 1971, p. 296.
25. See P. Sraffa, *Production of Commodities by Means of Commodities*, 1960, and Lady Robinson's writings *passim*. Lady Robinson herself seems to agree to this with regard to Dr. Sraffa's system, which she states 'exists in logical time, not in history', which *also* became her main charge against 'neo-classical' doctrines. (See *History versus Equilibrium*, 1974, p. 3.)
26. *Economics is a Serious Subject*, 1932, p. 6. Mrs. Robinson then took an extremely austere, even purist, view of the ambitions with which the economist should proceed, which perhaps it is a pity that she and other economists have in practice been quite disinclined explicitly to uphold: 'The economist must not be distressed at the accusation which the plain man brings against him that he is utterly heartless. The progress of physical science from the days of the Alchemists to the days when Doctor Cockcroft transmutes the elements in his laboratory was a circuitous one. And unless economics is content to remain for ever in the age of Alchemy it must *resolutely turn its back on the pursuit of gold, however precious it may be to human welfare*, and embark upon the path of an austere and disinterested search, not "for the Truth", but for a single self-consistent system of ideas.' (The dubious comparison with physics and chemistry may be noted as well as the setting up of the *purely logical* criterion of 'self-consistency'.) It should be noted also that the programme and criteria of 'optimistic' abstraction diverge completely from Marshall's programme for the study of firms and industries in terms of mainly empirical and historical investigations, as carried out in his great work on *Industry and Trade*. In fact, as Professor B. J. Loasby has observed, 'optimistic' imperfect competition analysis 'would now be generally regarded as one of the most notorious blind alleys in twentieth-century economics' (*Choice, Complexity and Ignorance*, 1976, p. 174).
27. J. Robinson, op. cit., pp. 7–10.
28. Compare the immediately preceding quotation from forty-one years earlier. See J. Robinson and J. Eatwell, *An Introduction to Modern Economics*, McGraw-Hill, 1973, p. 56. It may be noted that Lady Robinson and Mr. Eatwell are to be found

making full use of the assumption of adequate knowledge or correct expectations, after having earlier denounced this assumption as 'absurd' when employed by 'neo-classicals'. (Compare p. 40 and p. 178 of the above-cited volume.)

29. *Economics is a Serious Subject*, 1932, p. 10.

30. Op. cit., p. 10.

31. See *Essays in Political and Moral Philosophy*, 1888, p. 221.

32. See *Collected Writings of J. M. Keynes*, ed. E. Johnson, vol. XV, 1971, p. 44. The arbitrariness of Keynes's own assumptions about expectations is well brought out by J. A. Kregel, in 'Economic Methodology in the face of Uncertainty', *Economic Journal*, June 1976, p. 215.

33. See my article 'Expectations and Rational Conduct', *Zeitschrift für Nationalökonomie*, 1937, Band VIII, Heft 5, pp. 636 ff., and Chapter IV of *The Significance and Basic Postulates of Economic Theory*, 1938 and 1960.

34. 'All happy families resemble one another, but each unhappy family is unhappy in its own way.'

35. The rule attributed by Professor Lachmann to Cassel might seem perhaps unduly restrictive, 'that from the initial level of abstraction, however high, it must be possible gradually to approach reality by a sequence of approximations involving the modification of the initial assumptions', *if this were to be interpreted as requiring that 'reality' is somehow finally arrived at*. It would certainly exclude much of traditional and contemporary analysis. But this is a useful and to some extent essential question to pose regarding abstraction. (See L. M. Lachmann, *Macro-economic Thinking and the Market Economy*, I.E.A., 1973, p. 14.)

36. *Economica*, August 1973, pp. 322 ff. See also Professor Hahn's inaugural lecture, 'On the Notion of Equilibrium in Economics', 1973.

37. *Econometrica*, January 1970, pp. 1–3 (italics added).

38. *Economica*, August 1973, p. 322.

39. Op. cit. (italics added).

40. *On the Notion of Equilibrium in Economics*, 1973, p. 6.

41. *On the Notion of Equilibrium in Economics*, 1973, p. 14, and *Economica*, August 1973, p. 324 (italics added). GE 'theory', and these two articles, are brilliantly criticised in Professor B. J. Loasby's distinguished book, *Change, Complexity and*

Ignorance, 1976, which was published too late for me to take
properly into account. As Professor Loasby says: 'Hahn's
assertion that general equilibrium theorists have made "precise
an economic tradition which is two hundred years old"
demonstrates that he has very little idea what that tradition is
. . . As an attempt to provide a formal, rigorous explanation
of how resources are allocated in a market economy, general
equilibrium theory is a total failure' (pp. 47 and 62). Professor
Loasby aptly criticises 'this combination of fierce rigour in the
theory and unheeding slackness in its application' (p. 50).

42. *Economica*, August 1973, p. 324. I am indebted here to Mr. A.
Coddington's paper, 'The Rationale of General Equilibrium
Theory,' *Economic Inquiry*, Dec. 1975, p. 554 (though there
are important points on which I disagree with Mr. Coddington).

43. When Marshall gave a few lines in his *Principles* to 'the Giffen
paradox' (as it was later called), he did *not* do so because it was
simply a logically conceivable case, or *curiosum*, but because he
considered (rightly or wrongly) that there was serious *statistical
evidence* showing that, although the case was exceptional, it
was *empirically 'of importance'* for the behaviour of the poor.
(See *Principles of Economics*, 8th ed., 1920, p. 132.) Regarding
the logical possibility of multiple equilibria, it was given no
more than a footnote, and a footnote in an appendix, by Marshall.

44. *On the Notion of Equilibrium in Economics*, 1973, p. 14.
Elsewhere Professor Hahn tells us of 'the difficulty many
experience in understanding that an equilibrium theory in
general and the neo-classical theory in particular has nothing
causal to say. Such a theory cannot "tell us anything about the
history of the world".' Professor Hahn himself seems to
'experience difficulty' in understanding the full implications of
this statement and the limitations which it imposes. (v. *The
Share of Wages in National Income*, 1972, p. 3.)

45. *Economica*, August 1973, p. 324.

46. For example Ricardo writes to Malthus: 'I assume indeed that
nations in their commercial transactions *are so alive to their
advantage and profit*, particularly in the present improved state
of the division of employments and abundance of Capital, that in
point of fact money never does move but when it is advantageous
both to the country which sends and the country that receives
that it should do so. The first point to be considered is, what is

the interest of countries in the case supposed? The second what is their practise? Now it is obvious that *I need not be greatly solicitous about this latter point*; it is sufficient for my purpose if I can clearly demonstrate that the interest of the public is as I have stated. *It would be no answer to me to say that men were ignorant of the best and cheapest mode of conducting their business and paying their debts, because that is a question of fact not of science, and might be urged against almost every proposition in Political Economy.*' (*Works of D. Ricardo*, ed. P. Sraffa, vol. VI, 1952, p. 64, italics added.) This expresses the essence of Ricardian method: abstract model-building (with no need for being 'greatly solicitous' regarding the adequacy of the assumptions) and the opposing of 'questions of fact' to 'questions of science'. Again, in Chapter IV of *The Principles*, Ricardo reasons: 'While every man is free to employ his capital where he pleases, he will naturally seek for it that employment which is most advantageous; he will naturally be dissatisfied with a profit of 10 per cent., if by removing his capital he can obtain a profit of 15 per cent. . . . This . . . has a strong tendency to equalize the rate of profits of all.' This reasoning obviously only makes sense on the assumption of correct knowledge. (See also T. W. Hutchison, *The Significance and Basic Postulates of Economic Theory*, 1938 and 1960, pp. 85–6.)

47. The fatal fascination of abstractions is well described in a passage quoted by Professor Jacob Viner: 'In a lecture, sometimes in a book, we prefer even a false system, artificially and too ingeniously imposed upon the facts, to the subtleties and complications of truth, because it seems to offer us a clue to the labyrinth, a satisfying explanation in which our minds can rest, and an easily remembered formula. The mistaking of the appearance of system for profundity is one of the most persistent delusions of the human mind.' (P. Shorey, *Platonism Ancient and Modern*, 1938, p. 126, quoted by J. Viner, *Guide to John Rae's Life of Adam Smith*, 1965, p. 33.) This statement should be especially noted by 'Ricardians' of all types and stripes.

48. See the quotation above from Professor Hahn about how 'the vulgarizations of GE *which are the substance of most text-books on economics* are both scientifically and politically harmful' (italics added).

49. See *The Significance and Basic Postulates of Economic Theory*, 1938 and 1960, pp. 182–3; and H. Demsetz, 'Information and Efficiency, another viewpoint', *Journal of Law and Economics*, 1969, pp. 1 ff.

50. *Principles of Political Economy*, 2nd ed., 1836, p. 14.

51. Duncan Forbes, 'Sceptical Whiggism, Commerce and Liberty', in *Essays on Adam Smith*, ed. A. S. Skinner and T. Wilson, 1975, p. 201.

52. Letter to William Cullen, 20 September 1774, from *An Account of the Life; Lectures, and writings of William Cullen*, MD, by J. Thomson, 1859, vol. I, p. 189. I owe this reference to Mr. Michael Harvey Phillips.

53. See the very interesting paper, 'Economics, Economists and Economic Policy: Modern American Experiences', presented by Professor W. R. Allen to the Copenhagen Conference of the Economic History Society, 1974. Professor Allen quotes distinguished government economists as saying: 'The economic theory we are using is the theory most of us learned as sophomores.' And again: 'I think the economists' framework is the right one to weigh the advantages and disadvantages as best you can see them – but when economists sit down and prepare models to try to trace out these consequences in any sophisticated fashion, I think it's just about as apt to be misleading as it is to be helpful' (op. cit., pp. 13–14). I am grateful to Professor A. W. Coats for calling my attention to this paper.

54. *Economic Journal*, March 1972, pp. 2 and 9. The same suggestion regarding history was made in the Presidential Address to the Royal Economic Society (1974) by the considerably less critical Sir Donald MacDougall: 'I am told that applicants for some courses in economic history are obliged to show prior qualifications in econometrics. I would also like to see the reverse, *with economic history a compulsory subject for any student of econometrics*, to make him more aware of the complexities of the real world and show him that his data consists of more than time series' (*Economic Journal*, December 1974, p. 781).

55. *Economic Journal*, March 1972, p. 84. One need not agree with all Professor J. K. Galbraith's sometimes controversial views to appreciate the accuracy of his insight when he writes: 'There can be no question, however, that prolonged commitment to

mathematical exercises in economics can be damaging. It leads
to the atrophy of judgment and intuition which are indispensable
for real solutions and, on occasion, leads also to the habit of
mind which simply excludes the mathematically inconvenient
factors from consideration' (*A Contemporary Guide to
Economics, Peace and Laughter*, 1971, p. 41).

56. *History of Political Economy*, vol. 3, 1971, p. 233.

Chapter Five

1. Another evasive and obscurantist complaint, sometimes raised,
   is that quotations are 'taken out of context'. Almost by definition
   this could be said to be inevitably the case with a quotation.
   If taken literally this complaint could be used to justify the
   exclusion of all less-than-indefinitely-lengthy quotations.
   Of course quotations can be used to give a false impression, just
   as can statistical evidence. But those who try to ban quotation
   are encouraging uncritical obscurantism just as insidiously as
   those who would seek to ban statistical evidence because this can
   be misleadingly used.

2. The classical statement to the effect that to be regarded as a part
   of economic knowledge a theory or proposition must be widely
   or generally agreed by 'economists', is that of James Mill in his
   paper 'Whether Political Economy is Useful' (1836). Mill
   maintained that 'among those who have so much knowledge on
   the subject as to entitle their opinions to any weight, there is a
   wonderful agreement', regarding, that is, the propositions Mill
   himself (the methodological mentor of Ricardo) believed in
   (i.e. the 'Says Law' proposition; the natural wage and hard-line
   Malthusian proposition; a kind of labour cost 'theory' of value,
   etc.).

3. See *The Listener*, 4 May 1961, p. 763; *The London and
   Cambridge Economic Bulletin*, June 1962, p. 111; and
   The Times, 19 February–19 March 1963. I have given a fuller
   account of this discussion in *Economists and Economic Policy
   1946–1966*, 1968, pp. 219–22.

4. *Sterling in the Sixties*, Chatham House Essay, 1964, p. 59.

5. Messrs. Hambro and Warburg were strongly supported in
   The Sunday Times the next day by Mr. W. Rees-Mogg in an
   article headed 'Why devaluation is no solution to the crisis'.
   Five years later, however, combining hindsight and myth, a

Sunday Times editorial was proclaiming that 'sterling devaluation would have been the right course in 1964', and that Mr. Wilson's orthodoxy in clinging to the sterling parity was 'strongly challenged' in 1964 (*Sunday Times*, 10 August 1969, p. 10). I owe the reference to Mr. Rees-Mogg's article to Professor D. J. Coppock, *Manchester School*, September 1965, p. 296.

6. Of course government economists were not free to publish their views. Moreover, as has been suggested by Mr. Peter Oppenheimer, some economists who favoured devaluation at that time *may*, like himself, have had their contribution refused by editors. Clearly support for devaluation might have been excluded from *The New Statesman*, for example. But anyone feeling strongly on the subject could presumably have got a letter published in *The Observer*.

7. *Crisis in the Civil Service*, ed. H. Thomas, 1968, p. 56 (italics added). Just previously Mr. Opie had put it the other way round explaining that in October 1964 'the political conditions could not have been more suitable or the economic less so' for a devaluation (*New Statesman*, 24 November 1967, p. 703).

8. See the editorial in *The Bankers' Magazine*, December 1964, p. 340. Mr. Opie was engaged in denouncing, on the lines developed by Messrs. Hahn and Little, the moral and economic attack on devaluation by Messrs. Hambro and Warburg in *The Times* (see above), in which Mr. Opie himself was strongly supporting the import surcharge (18 and 27 November).
Mr. Opie's only other editorial comment on devaluation seems to have been in May 1963 when he proclaimed that 'devaluation is a dead duck as a policy' (*The Bankers' Magazine*, May 1963, p. 403). Mr. Opie has explained changes of view on devaluation in terms of religious conversion: 'For each man it was simply a private discovery of God' (*Sunday Times*, 26 November 1967, p. 31).

9. *The Pound Sterling: a Polemic*, 1965, p. 54 (italics added).

10. Op. cit., pp. 15–16.

11. Op. cit., pp. 78 and 80.

12. Op. cit., p. 66.

13. Op. cit., pp. 64–6.

14. Authoritative general support for exchange-rate variations came in February 1965 from Professor G. Haberler in his *Money in*

M

the International Economy, Hobert Paper No. 31, pp. 43–6. On the other hand Professor J. Viner had just previously argued strongly against floating rates: 'A perfectly floating exchange is probably an inconceivable thing, if one defines it strictly. . . I still feel that a wide range of countries – and in this range I include the United States, with qualifications – are not safely to be trusted with a floating exchange; and that the fixed-exchange rate – cult, myth, rigidity, illogicality though it may be – is in many countries, the sole surviving barrier to almost unrestrained inflation.' (*Problems of Monetary Control*, Princeton, May 1964, pp. 31–4.)

15. Professor Triffin wrote: 'Although currency devaluation might, as a consequence, become inescapable at some point, it could hardly be regarded as desirable. On the contrary, the temporary respite which it would bring about might relieve useful pressures for overdue structural adaptations in many sectors of British industry.' (*The Banker*, February 1965, p. 81.)

16. *National Institute Economic Review*, August 1965, p. 18. See also *The Times*, 20 August 1965.

17. *Manchester School*, September 1965, p. 294.

18. *How to Stop Stop-Go*, 1966, pp. 13 and 30–4. Mr. Williamson recommended a devaluation of 6–7 per cent over the next 3½ years and the introduction of a system of 'crawling pegs'. He estimated that 1¾ per cent unemployment would provide an adequate measure of spare capacity: 'We do not need to accept a target for unemployment so depressing as Paish's 2¼ per cent.' Mr. Williamson argued that it was high time (December 1965) that the deflationary measures were cautiously reversed 'if the danger of recession in 1966 and 1967 is to be averted'. In an introduction to this pamphlet (p. 1) Mr. C. Layton seemed to present devaluation as a kind of article of faith or rallying cry for an economic *Jugendbewegung*, believed in 'by most economists, of whatever party, under the age of 40'.

19. *Scottish Journal of Political Economy*, February 1966, pp. 21–2, 134, & 3.

20. In addition to *The Bankers' Magazine*, *The Banker*, edited by Mr. W. King, expressed opposition to devaluation during this period. See for example the comment in November 1964 (p. 685) that 'Mr. Wilson . . . wisely turned his back on the mirage of devaluation'.

21. As Professor Kaldor put it: 'The White Paper published on October 26, 1964, 10 days after the new Government took office, undoubtedly shows that full extent of the internal pressure of demand was not immediately appreciated.' Professor Kaldor seems to have been the only economist advising or supporting the Government who had, from the time of the budget in April, recognised and warned of the dangers of 'an unjustified boom calling for urgent restraint' – though the National Institute in its *Review* of May had concluded with a similar warning. (See Professor Kaldor's letters to *The Times* of 28 July 1964 and of 23 and 25 April 1970; also his letter of 8 June 1970, where he adds that 'this unhealthy and unsustainable situation was only partly due to the overvaluation of the pound. It was also a reflection of unsound public finance.')

22. E.g. 'The greater equality implied by tax-reform will provide the basis for a national incomes policy' (T. Balogh, *New Statesman*, 25 September 1964, p. 434).

23. *After the Boom*, September 1966, pp. 21–2.

24. *Economics: An Awkward Corner*, 1966, pp. 20 and 30.

25. *Hansard, House of Lords Debates*, 28 July 1966. Lord Robbins had also opposed devaluation in the House of Lords about a year previously on 4 August 1965. Lord Robbins was one of the very few economists who emphasised a moral element, of responsibilities to creditors, in the devaluation issue.

26. *Though Cowards Flinch*, 1967, p. 52 (italics added). See also his article in *The Spectator*, 29 July 1966 (p. 140): 'Any unemployment created after devaluation will quickly disappear as the production of goods for export increases.'

27. Op. cit., p. 40.

28. *New Statesman*, 3 March 1967, p. 280. However *The New Statesman* continued its editorial opposition to devaluation *as late as September 1967* when it strongly condemned both a fiscal 'squeeze' and devaluation, putting all the emphasis on an incomes 'freeze': 'It is no reply to say that devaluation would be an easy way out. Without an incomes freeze devaluation would fail. With a freeze devaluation would be unnecessary. . . Both the squeeze and devaluation stand condemned' (15 September 1967, p. 306). Later (*New Statesman*, 22 May 1970, p. 720) Mr. Opie described the Labour Government as having 'with the full support of *The Times*, poured its energies

and the country's gold reserves' into maintaining the exchange
rate. One must add, of course, 'with the full support of
The New Statesman', as far as maintaining the exchange rate
is concerned.

29. *Towards a New Economic Policy*, 1967, pp. 22 and 29. An
honorary degree citation is perhaps not always the most
rigorously accurate kind of authority on which to rely. But one
may fully credit the statement of the Public Orator of the
University of Warwick, when presenting Sir Roy in June 1968,
that 'he regarded devaluation, both in 1949 and 1967 as idiotic'
(*University of Warwick Gazette*, October 1968, p. 7).

30. *The Bankers' Magazine*, April 1967, pp. 225 ff. Mr. Scott had a
year previously given a rather less cautious and less detailed
exposition of the case for devaluation, or, more particularly, for
devaluation followed by a controlled flexible rate, in an essay on
'The Balance of Payments', in *Economic Growth in Britain*,
ed. P. D. Henderson, 1966, pp. 85 ff.

31. Op. cit., pp. 230–4 (italics added).

32. *Verbatim Report of an Economic Seminar*, 1967, p. 43.
Mr. Farrell maintained that 'something must be done about the
exchange rate sooner or later and my own hope is that it will be
sooner' (p. 11). Professor Pyatt remarked that 'if we were going
to devalue the pound now would perhaps be quite a good time'
(p. 13).

33. *New Statesman*, 17 November 1967, p. 644 (italics added).

34. *New Statesman*, 24 November 1967, p. 703 (italics added).
Mr. S. Brittan has observed: 'Devaluation only became an
important "left-wing" cause just before and after it actually
happened. . . It was the more "left-wing" of the Labour
Government's economic advisers, who took longest to come
round to devaluation.' (*Left or Right, the Bogus Dilemma*,
1968, pp. 22–3.) In contrast with *The New Statesman* which
had for so long opposed devaluation and then wrote in terms of
imminent miracles when it was finally forced on the Government (while soon after demanding the resignation of Mr.
Jenkins), the *Spectator* (24 November 1967), which had for some
time advocated devaluation, was very sceptical of the Government's ability or will to make it successful.

35. *Observer*, 26 November 1967, p. 12. A fortnight previously,
before devaluation, Professor Day had been rather more

optimistic: 'If we were prepared to change the exchange rate, we could rapidly create the export-led boom of which there are no signs at present. This would reduce unemployment to a reasonable level.' (*Observer*, 12 November 1967, p. 10.)

36. According to Mr. S. Brittan (*Left or Right: The Bogus Dilemma*, 1968, p. 69): 'After the 1967 devaluation there was a considerable consensus about what had to be done to make devaluation work among those who understood the subject.' The consensus among economists did not last very long and was never very extensive.

37. *The* UK *Economy, a Manual of Applied Economics*, ed. A. R. Prest, 2nd edition, 1968, pp. 87 and 115–23 (italics added).

38. Optimism was further encouraged at this juncture by the Brookings Institution Study of *Britain's Economic Prospects* which found (p. 488) 'the 14.3% reduction in the external value of the pound more than adequate to restore equilibrium', while Professor R. N. Cooper had concluded his essay on the balance of payments with the prediction (p. 197) that 'the devaluation should leave Britain's payments position — and the objectives that underlie it — much firmer than during the preceding decade'.

39. Later, Lord Balogh maintained that 'the hard slog has not even begun. Real consumption, far from falling in 1968, has increased by some 2½ per cent.' (*Sunday Times*, 16 March 1969, p. 12.) Subsequently, however, Mr. A. Graham and Professor W. Beckerman maintained that 'it is only with hindsight that one can see that the cumulative deflation in 1968 and 1969 was too large'. (See *The Labour Government's Economic Record 1964–1970*, ed. W. Beckerman, 1972, p. 24.)

40. *New Statesman*, 1 November 1968, p. 569 (italics added). This theme was repeated in a *New Statesman* editorial of 6 June 1969 headed 'Thorneycroft Rides Again', according to which Mr. Thorneycroft 'pursued his orthodoxy almost up to his 1958 budget when Prime Minister Macmillan's political antennae sensed the madness of cutting government expenditure in such an environment. He was right. Thorneycroft resigned, and the country and the government was saved.' Actually the 1958 budget of Mr. Heathcoat Amory was *not* expansionist. Mr. Macmillan's political antennae, and the highly expansionist 1959 budget, may have 'saved the government' in helping it to win the general election of October 1959 and to renew its hold

on office: whether measures of this kind 'saved the *country*' seems doubtful. That office for a particular party must be the overriding objective of economic policy, was the assumption on which these arguments rested.

41. *Observer*, 18 May 1969, p. 8. Presumably what was political suicide in 1969 would have been at least somewhat rash in 1964–5, with a single-figure majority for the Government.

42. *New Statesman*, 4 July 1969, p. 4 (some italics added).

43. R. Opie in *Crisis in the Civil Service*, ed. H. Thomas, 1968, p. 57.

44. *The Times Annual Financial and Economic Review*, 30 September 1969.

45. *Financial Times*, 18 November 1969.

46. See *New Statesman*, 3 March, 22 May, 17 and 31 July 1970 (italics added). Mr. Opie, however, was not entirely pessimistic, proclaiming that the selective employment tax 'probably is one among many factors which will generate the British productivity miracle of the 1970s'. Similar optimism was also soon after forthcoming from Professor Lord Vaizey: 'President Nixon and Mr. Heath have all the luck. They are in office at the beginning of a long secular upward trend, and they will both be able to claim some merit for what will happen. . . My growing optimism, periodically recorded in these pages has been justified.' (*Sunday Telegraph*, 22 August 1971, p. 21.)

47. *New Statesman*, 22 February and 1 March 1974.

48. *New Statesman*, 1 March 1974. The Budgets so praised by Lord Kaldor were, of course, those that had been so scathingly denounced in the same paper a few brief years earlier. Conventional 'go-go' wisdom was also well represented, as often, in *The Times Literary Supplement* (6 October 1972): 'Certainly Roy Jenkins' budgets dealing with the devaluation were grossly misconceived; indeed he was a veritable Snowden among Chancellors.' Incidentally, when Lord Kaldor praises the budgets of 'the Snowden among Chancellors' for 'providing resources', he is using a euphemism for what is sometimes called the 'redeployment of labour', which is, in turn, a euphemism for 'adding to unemployment'. Of course, additional unemployment in the short run is advocated in order to raise the level and wages of employment in the longer run (a by no means unjustifiable strategy).

49. *Crisis in the Civil Service*, ed. H. Thomas, 1968, p. 60.
50. See *Economists and the Economic Policy 1964–1966*, 1968, pp. 207–33. We have drawn here, for a few sentences, on a review which appeared in *Economica*, May 1973, p. 222. See also P. Sinclair in *The Decade of Disillusion*, ed. D. McKie and C. Cook, 1972, pp. 94 and 103: 'For the British economy, the sixties were years of bitter disappointment. The real failure of Governments lay not so much in their economic policies as in their extravagant claims of omnicompetence. A credulous public was led to expect El Dorado, found only plenty, and became understandably dissatisfied. . . Much vaunted economic expertise failed to bring home the goods that some Governments were foolish enough to predict. . . *The impression brilliantly conveyed to the electorate in 1964 was that some undefined negative attitude implicit in 'stop-go' and some unspecified kind of governmental amateurism were all that had deprived Britain of rapid growth in the fifties and early sixties. Purposive and dynamic government would suddenly restore her rightful rate of growth*' (italics added). The essential element here is the alliance between 'much vaunted economic expertise' and political vote-winning, – the formula for what might be described as 'honours-list', or 'life-peerage economics'. As has been sharply observed: 'The professional politicians would dearly love the economists to tell them certain things. It is said that the way to a man's heart is through his stomach. But there is no surer way to a politician's heart than to tell him he can safely do things which are sure vote-winners. And when you've got his heart, prestige, power, and if you're lucky a knighthood, are not far away.' (T. Arthur, *Ninety-Five Per Cent is Crap*, 1975, p. 184.)
51. 'It is not only people's hopes that have been dashed; it is their confidence in all those to whom they have entrusted the conduct of their affairs and, even more perhaps, in that great army of experts who, in think-tanks all over the world, assiduously poured out blueprints of the future which, however much they might vary from each other, at least agreed in this: that there was no limit to the continuous increase in the production of material goods to which we could all confidently look for-ward. . . Where are they now, those prophets of continually multiplying gross national products, those hordes of scientists,

economists . . . who, like flocks of migratory birds, filled the air?' (v. 'Column', *Encounter*, January 1975, p. 35.)

52. R. Opie in *Crisis in the Civil Service*, ed. H. Thomas, 1968, pp. 59–63.

53. *The New Statesman*, 22 May 1970.

54. M. Stewart, *Encounter*, May 1968, p. 56 (italics added).

55. P. Streeten and M. Lipton, *Times Literary Supplement*, 20 June 1968, p. 661 (italics added). See below for the subsequent (1972) views of one of the Government's senior advisers (Lord Balogh).

56. W. Beckerman, *The Labour Government's Economic Record 1964–70*, p. 61 (italics added).

57. Anon., *Times Literary Supplement*, 6 October 1972, p. 1191 (italics added).

58. These political implications have, however, been held to be of considerable significance: 'It is essential to have this mistake fully documented and demonstrated because, if correct, it is potentially a major alibi for much of the failure of policies in so many other economic and non-economic directions. If growth, planning, full employment, incomes policies and industrial reorganisation policies – to say nothing of aid, school-building, hospital building, welfare provision etc., only failed because of a wilful and gratuitous refusal to dispose of the balance of payments problem by the available means of devaluation, then the charges against these policies must at least be still regarded as unproven.' (P. Jay in *The Times*, 7 April 1972, p. 14.)

59. The classical example of this propensity is to be found in the essay by James Mill, the mentor and tutor of Ricardo, on 'Whether Political Economy is Useful'. See *James Mill, Selected Economic Writings*, ed. D. Winch, 1966, pp. 371 ff.

60. Professor W. Beckerman, *New Statesman*, 24 April 1972. Mr. Harold Lever then answered: 'He appears to have assumed the role of a Pythagoras of exchange rate theory, claiming for his position the same scientific certitude as those able to demonstrate that the world is round' (12 May 1972). Asserting the flatness of the earth was exactly what J. A. Hobson was accused of when he began to question 'classical' orthodoxy regarding effective demand in 1889 – and lost posts in London and Oxford, apparently as a consequence.

61. Among the 'flat-earthers' between 1964 and 1967 were

C. W. McMahon (1964); R. Opie (December 1964); M. Hurst (December 1964); R. Triffin (February 1965); M. Posner (July 1965); D. C. Rowan (February 1966); Lord Robbins (August 1965 and July 1966); Sir John Hicks (September 1966); Sir Roy Harrod (1967 and repeatedly); R. J. Ball (April and July 1967); and P. Bareau (July 1967).

62. 'Another Autopsy on Britain's Balance of Payments: 1958–1967', *Banca Nazionale del Lavoro Quarterly Review*, September 1970, pp. 16–19.

63. *Essays in Honour of Lord Robbins*, ed. M. Peston and B. Corry, 1972, p. 199.

64. *New Society*, 4 May 1972, p. 245 (italics added). See also *Fact and Fancy in International Economic Relations*, 1973, where it is claimed that 'the "success" of the British devaluation of 1967, after 1970 is mainly attributable to inflation abroad', while it 'proved the "elasticity-mongers" completely wrong' (pp. 93—4).

65. However, according to the diary of Mr. R. H. S. Crossman for 24 November 1966, Lord Balogh was then advising that devaluation 'was the only thing left and should be got over as soon as possible'. (See *The Diaries of a Cabinet Minister*, vol. I, 1975, p. 71, and pp. 204, 221, 305 and 572.) For Lord Balogh's views on the 1949 devaluation see my *Economists and Economic Policy 1946–1966*, 1968, pp. 77–9.

66. Contrast the judgment of Mr. R. Opie in *The New Statesman* at the time (24 November 1967) that the devaluation 'was a copy book performance' . . . 'made in the right conditions accompanied by the right supporting measures' . . . and 'shown to be the right amount' (see above, p. 121).

67. See *Review of Britain's Economic Prospects*, February 1975, p. 9; R. Neild, *The Times*, 27 February 1975, and S. Brittan, *Financial Times*, 27 February 1975. As Professor Neild, one of the leading proposers of devaluation in the early sixties now emphasised: 'Our freedom to devalue repeatedly is circumscribed by many factors. . . *Except in conditions very favourable to wage stability* – which we do not now enjoy – the stimulus it provides tends quickly to be eroded away by the inflation it generates' (*The Times*, 23 April 1975, italics added). Similarly, from a diametrically contrasting monetary-theoretical viewpoint, it was proclaimed by Professor M. Parkin that '*exchange rates*

are largely irrelevant. Variations in them have no lasting effect on anything *except* the price level of the country concerned' (*The Banker*, p. 1142, quoted by T. Wilson, in *Effective Devaluation and Inflation*, University of Glasgow Discussion Paper, 1975, p. 1). Professor Parkin described this as the 'new monetarist view'.

The new monetarist case against devaluation has also been very recently stated by Professor H. G. Johnson (*Banca Nazionale del Lavaro, Quarterly Review*, March 1976, p. 17): 'Devaluation is only capable of improving the balance of payments temporarily, and then only if it is backed up by a restrictive monetary policy. Consequently, we should not be surprised that much of the evidence about devaluations seems to suggest that they often do not work – the wrong theory of devaluation leads to looking for the wrong evidence and misinterpreting it when you find it. . . There is some justification for treating devaluation as a last-resort policy, because of the economically disturbing side-effects of the associated inflation, rather than treating it as the *sine qua non* of freedom of domestic policy action.' These conclusions seem to be in some contrast with Professor Johnson's earlier views when he alleged that the case against devaluation in Britain after 1964 went largely by default, and that this failure exemplified the unscientific, 'forensic' character of economics and economists in England as contrasted with the U.S., 'the homeland of scientific economics', where 'by contrast, there has always been, since the balance of payments deficit became a serious problem, a vocal group of academic advocates of devaluation' (*Encounter*, May 1968, p. 51). Economics is a subject where a 'forensic' tortoise may sometimes seem to be ahead of a 'scientific' hare.

68. Of course some economists have been quoted more often and at much greater length than others, *roughly in accordance with how often and how much they published on this subject.* It would *not* be representative to quote all economists the same number of times or at the same length, nor to follow some ranking order of one's own in deciding how much, or how often to quote from any particular economist.

69. 'In the last resort the correct rate is a technical matter' (M. Stewart, *Encounter*, May 1968, p. 56).

70. *Papers Relating to Political Economy*, vol. I, 1925, p. 8.
71. *The Observer*, 24 October 1971.
72. *The Listener*, 15 July 1971.
73. *New Statesman*, 18 May 1973 (italics added).
74. In 1963 Lord Kaldor had especially emphasised the alternatives to entering the EEC: 'If we do not give up our independence . . . we could raise our economic strength considerably by a vigorous policy of comprehensive economic planning. . . The Common-wealth, as an association, is gaining added strength through the accession of the many newly emergent countries of Asia, Africa and the Caribbean. . . The true nature of the motives and interests which caused the wave of enthusiasm for the Common Market . . . was the fear of British socialism. . . The whole issue is being rapidly forgotten.' (v. *Encounter*, March 1963, p. 73: *New Statesman*, 26 July 1963, and my *Economists and Economic Policy, 1946–1966*, 1968, p. 206.)

    Professor H. G. Johnson maintained: 'The obvious economic benefits to Britain of joining the EEC are negligible, and the obvious economic costs are large' (*Spectator*, 13 February 1971).
75. 'The Common Market Questionnaire, October 1971', by M. S. Khan and H. G. Johnson, *Economica*, August 1972, pp. 316 ff. A poll of 'Business Economists' taken independently showed 176 judging the economic effects of entry to be favour-able and 36 against (see a letter from Mr. T. M. Rybczynski in *The Times*, 28 October 1971).
76. Op. cit., p. 317 (italics added).
77. Professor A. W. Coats has given the total number of 'academic posts' in economics in 1969 as 1802 (v. an unpublished paper on 'The Development of the Economics Profession in England'). So the response rate *may* not have been more than about 20–30 per cent.
78. G. Hallett, *The Times*, 27 October 1971.

Index of Names